A Woman's Influential Relationships

Book 3

Unlimited!... Bible Studies for Today's Pentecostal Woman

Arlene Allen, Peggy Musgrove,
Lori O'Dea, & Candy Tolbert

GPH
Gospel Publishing House
Springfield, Missouri
02-0277

CONTENTS

FOREWORD

Nothing is more important than relationships. Our relationship with God is the primary concern, and our relationships with family members, coworkers, the church community, and friends can support and encourage us or tear us apart. Who wouldn't enjoy picking up a vibrant Bible study on this topic? Talk about applicable!

As women, we are designed to thrive on positive connections in our lives. We are meant to laugh and cry together, to share our frustrations and our victories. We are called to tell people about the most meaningful relationship we have—our relationship with Jesus. How can we share the message effectively?

In this third book, developed specifically for women, you will find discussions about women in Scripture who learned some interesting lessons about relationships. You will read about people like Elizabeth, Phoebe, Naomi, and even some women whose names we do not know, like the woman at the well and the widow with the oil. You see, even when we feel like no one knows us or understands what we are going through, God is aware.

These Bible studies focus on 2 Timothy. You can study the lessons by yourself if you want, but since this is all about relationships, how about gathering a couple of women together and chatting about the lessons over a nice cup of coffee? There's hardly any better way to learn and grow than to hear the ideas someone else has about the same text you're studying.

The four authors of this book are remarkable women. Arlene Allen is the director for the national Women's Ministries Department of the Assemblies of God. Peggy Musgrove once held that position and is now a speaker and freelance writer. Dr. Lori O'Dea served on several pastoral staffs before she became the Doctor of Ministry Coordinator and

Visiting Professor of Practical Theology for the Assemblies of God Theological Seminary. Candy Tolbert is the national leadership development coordinator for the Women's Ministries Department of the Assemblies of God. All four are active, successful writers and teachers and, with their accumulated experience in ministry, family, and church relationships, their wisdom will leap off these pages.

You will want to be part of this relevant Bible study. You'll grow as these women of the "now" bring to life some amazing women of the Bible and change the way you think about relationships. Enjoy the journey.

Carolyn Tennant
Professor of English
North Central University
Minneapolis, Minnesota

PREFACE

This series of Bible studies was written in response to women and pastors across the United States who have asked for Pentecostal studies to use in their churches for group or individual study.

A Woman's Influential Relationships is a Pentecostal study written by Pentecostal women. This study is unique to any you have used before because the Pentecostal perspective is written into each lesson. The student will not have to search for the Pentecostal viewpoint—she needs only to embrace it and ask Jesus to help her apply it.

The Bible describes two types of relationships: vertical and horizontal. Our primary relationship is with God—all other relationships flow from it. In the Scriptures, relational problems increased as fast as the earth's population did. Adam and Eve refused to accept responsibility for their sin, thus hurting their relationship with God; Cain murdered his brother, Abel, in a fit of rage; Sarah mistreated her slave, Hagar; Jacob stole Esau's birthright; Laban cheated Jacob; and Joseph's brothers sold him into slavery. These are just a few examples of flawed relationships from the first book of the Bible.

These lessons will help you build right relationships, and learn the importance of restoring broken relationships. Within healthy relationships, we receive support, encouragement, acceptance, help, and love. However, in a bad relationship, we can experience rejection, judgment, discouragement, insensitivity, and jealousy.

Our prayer is that these studies will help you rejoice in your healthy relationships and examine your flawed relationships, giving you a renewed determination to heal them.

Arlene Allen
Director, Women's Ministries Department
General Council of the Assemblies of God

Her Relationship to God

CATCHING SIGHT

Introduction

WHO DOESN'T LIKE to make tracks in fresh snow? It is great fun for boys and girls. And many grown-ups enjoy plodding in the snow—at least until they get out of breath!

Two little boys were enjoying the first heavy snowfall of winter. They threw snowballs, made several snowmen, and rolled a big snowball until it was so large they couldn't push it any farther. Then one of the boys said, "Let's see who can make the straightest tracks across that field."

Over a fence they went as they started across the field. When they got to the other side of the field and looked back, they saw one set of tracks that made an almost-straight path across the field and another set of tracks that zigzagged.

Why was one set of tracks straight and the other zigzag? The boy who walked the straight line picked out a fence post on the other side of the field and kept his eyes on it, always walking straight toward it. The other boy hadn't focused on a specific target and as a result, he wandered from a straight path.

To build a relationship with God, we need to fix our eyes on Him as we journey through life. The more time we spend with Him in prayer and in His Word, the better we will know Him and the deeper our relationship with Him will become.

GETTING FOCUSED
Begin your study by considering the following:

What components make up a good relationship? Are any of these missing in your relationship with God?

BIBLE READING
2 Timothy 1:1–14

New International Version

1 Paul, an apostle of Christ Jesus by the will of God, according to the promise of life that is in Christ Jesus, 2 To Timothy, my dear son: Grace, mercy and peace from God the Father and Christ Jesus our Lord.

3 I thank God, whom I serve, as my forefathers did, with a clear conscience, as night and day I constantly remember you in my prayers. 4 Recalling your tears, I long to see you, so that I may be filled with joy. 5 I have been reminded of your sincere faith, which first lived in your grandmother Lois and in your mother Eunice and, I am persuaded, now lives in you also. 6 For this reason I remind you to fan into flame the gift of God, which is in you through the laying on of my hands. 7 For God did not give us a spirit of timidity, but a spirit of power, of love and of self-discipline.

8 So do not be ashamed to testify about our Lord, or ashamed of me his prisoner. But join with me in suffering for the gospel, by the power of God, 9 who has saved us and called

New Living Translation

1 This letter is from Paul, an apostle of Christ Jesus by God's will, sent out to tell others about the life he has promised through faith in Christ Jesus.

2 It is written to Timothy, my dear son. May God our Father and Christ Jesus our Lord give you grace, mercy, and peace.

3 Timothy, I thank God for you. He is the God I serve with a clear conscience, just as my ancestors did. Night and day I constantly remember you in my prayers. 4 I long to see you again, for I remember your tears as we parted. And I will be filled with joy when we are together again.

5 I know that you sincerely trust the Lord, for you have the faith of your mother, Eunice, and your grandmother, Lois. 6 This is why I remind you to fan into flames the spiritual gift God gave you when I laid my hands on you. 7 For God has not given us a spirit of fear and timidity, but of power, love, and self-discipline. 8 So you must never be ashamed to tell others about our

New International Version

us to a holy life—not because of anything we have done but because of his own purpose and grace. This grace was given us in Christ Jesus before the beginning of time, 10 but it has now been revealed through the appearing of our Savior, Christ Jesus, who has destroyed death and has brought life and immortality to light through the gospel. 11 And of this gospel I was appointed a herald and an apostle and a teacher. 12 That is why I am suffering as I am. Yet I am not ashamed, because I know whom I have believed, and am convinced that he is able to guard what I have entrusted to him for that day.

13 What you heard from me, keep as the pattern of sound teaching, with faith and love in Christ Jesus. 14 Guard the good deposit that was entrusted to you—guard it with the help of the Holy Spirit who lives in us.

New Living Translation

Lord. And don't be ashamed of me, either, even though I'm in prison for Christ. With the strength God gives you, be ready to suffer with me for the proclamation of the Good News.

9 It is God who saved us and chose us to live a holy life. He did this not because we deserved it, but because that was his plan long before the world began—to show his love and kindness to us through Christ Jesus. 10 And now he has made all of this plain to us by the coming of Christ Jesus, our Savior, who broke the power of death and showed us the way to everlasting life through the Good News. 11 And God chose me to be a preacher, an apostle, and a teacher of this Good News.

12 And that is why I am suffering here in prison. But I am not ashamed of it, for I know the one in whom I trust, and I am sure that he is able to guard what I have entrusted to him until the day of his return.

13 Hold on to the pattern of right teaching you learned from me. And remember to live in the faith and love that you have in Christ Jesus. 14 With the help of the Holy Spirit who lives within us, carefully guard what has been entrusted to you.

GAINING BIBLICAL INSIGHT
Yielding my life to God

We can tell the kind of relationship we have with another person by the number of times that person's name comes up in our conversations. Doting grandparents find ways to insert stories about their grandchildren in almost any conversation. Young lovers can turn any topic to include reference to the object of their affection.

From Paul's writings to his "son" Timothy, we learn how important his relationship with the Lord was. God's name appears in almost every sentence of the epistle. By studying these references, we begin to understand Paul's relationship with God.

When we understand how much Paul loved God, we gain insight into his relationships with people. His life illustrates the basic Christian principles of loving God with all our heart, soul, strength, and mind, and loving others as ourselves.

The Foundation of Paul's Relationship with God

Though Paul had been schooled in Judaism from birth, his new relationship with God began dramatically on the Damascus Road. This experience redefined his life.

In his opening statement (verse 1), Paul calls himself an *apostle*, a title that reveals his radical change of lifestyle from a persecutor of believers to a proclaimer of truth. He moved from one who "breath[ed] out murderous threats against the Lord's disciples" (Acts 9:1) to one who would risk his life for the gospel. His conversion experience truly revolutionized his life.

According to his opening statement, Paul understood that his apostleship was based on the "promise of life that is in Christ Jesus." He encountered reality in Christ on the Damascus Road. This encounter was the foundational experience of Paul's lifetime walk with God.

What was your first encounter with the gospel? Was it as radical as Paul's Damascus Road experience? Or was your decision to follow Christ the result of early training?

How has your decision to follow Christ affected your lifestyle?

How we come to faith in Christ is not as important as knowing we have established a relationship with Him, based on the promise of His Word.

The Manifestation of Paul's Relationship with God

Continue reading verses 3–5. Look at the characteristics of Paul's relationship with God. Note first of all his grateful spirit as he prayerfully expresses thanksgiving for memories of Timothy. Our experience with God should produce gratitude in our hearts, not only for our own experience with God, but also for our relationships with family and friends in Christ.

If you would thank God for another Christian today, who would that be? Pause a minute to do so, and to pray for that person, just as Paul prayed for Timothy.

Paul valued the gifts and graces of God he recognized in Christian friends. In verse 6, he encouraged Timothy to "fan into flame the gift of God," because Paul valued what God values.

Paul reminded Timothy that the spirit of fear does not come from God—God gives the spirit of power, of love, and of self-discipline (verse 7). Paul must have experienced these gifts in his own life as a result of his relationship with God, because he spoke with assurance in his exhortation to Timothy.

From verses 8–12 we learn Paul was able to endure suffering for the gospel by the grace and power of God. His relationship with God gave him assurance that God was working in spite of the problems Paul was experiencing. His knowledge of God gave him confidence in God's keeping power.

The Challenge of Paul's Relationship with God

Paul charged Timothy to remember what he had been taught, using these lessons as a pattern for life. The same lessons also serve as a pattern for us. The most important relationship we will ever have is our relationship with God. Our challenge is to follow Paul's example.

Meditate a few moments on 2 Timothy 1:12. Our relationship with God begins when we can say with Paul, "I know whom I have believed" with full assurance in our hearts. Having established that relationship, we commit ourselves completely to Him as Paul did, determining we will keep the faith, no matter what happens.

If you have made this decision, pause a moment to reaffirm your commitment. If you have not done so, now would be a good time to start your relationship with Him by affirming with Paul your belief in Jesus Christ, asking Him to forgive you of all sins which separate you from Him. Then commit yourself to wholly following Him. To strengthen that commitment, share your decision with a friend.

This would be a more difficult decision to follow through with if we were trying to make it on our own. But, as Paul tells us in verse 14, we have the help of the Holy Spirit who lives in us. We do not live the Christian life in our own strength, but we draw daily on the power of the Holy Spirit to keep us committed.

When our relationship with God is firm, we are ready to build relationships with His people. To love others deeply, we must first love God. Paul's relationship with Timothy was an outgrowth of his vibrant relationship with God.

Amazing things happen in the lives of people who commit themselves fully to God. Two such people in the Bible were Zechariah and Elizabeth, devout servants of the Lord. Listen as Elizabeth tells her story of God's miraculous work in their lives.

REFLECTING HIS IMAGE
Elizabeth (Luke 1:24,25)

Elizabeth was confused and a little frightened when her husband came through the door and gestured for her to sit down. *What has happened?* she wondered. *Is he hurt? He looks confused. Why doesn't he say something?*

She knew *something* extraordinary had taken place as she joined him at the table. Moments later, her confusion turned to relief and joy when Zechariah communicated in sign language the events of the day.

He was carrying out his priestly duties as the congregation gathered to pray outside the temple. Unannounced, an angel of God appeared just to the right of the altar of incense. Zechariah was paralyzed in fear.

The angel reassured him, "Don't fear, Zechariah. Your prayer has been heard. Elizabeth, your wife, will bear a son by you. You are to name him John . . . . He'll achieve great stature with God."[1]

Elizabeth sat motionless and the room was eerily quiet as Zechariah continued signing. "When I returned to my congregation, I couldn't speak and they all knew I'd seen a vision. That's when I began to use sign language with my people."

As her eyes widened and her mind raced, Elizabeth thought, *Amazing! No, miraculous!* Looking deep into her husband's face, she exclaimed, "We're going to have a baby! At our age, we're going to have a baby!" For years, they had both prayed and longed for a child. Now they were well past the age for childbearing. Yet, a miracle was happening.

Though childless, Elizabeth was a woman who loved God and was faithful to her husband. Smiling now, she remembered a favorite story of fulfillment in the Scripture. Abraham fell facedown; he laughed and said to himself, "Will a son be born to a man a hundred years old? Will Sarah bear a child at the age of ninety? Then God said 'Your wife Sarah will bear you a son, and you will call him Isaac.'"[2]

Lovingly, she reached across the table and gently squeezed her husband's hand. "Zechariah," she said, "If it happened to Sarah, it can happen to me. A son! Amazing."

Six months passed and Elizabeth's cousin, Mary, came to pay a visit. "You look wonderful," Mary said as they embraced. Before Elizabeth could respond, the baby within her jumped. She exclaimed, "You're so blessed among women, and the babe in your womb, also blessed!"[3]

Elizabeth and Zechariah had read Isaiah: "A girl who is presently a virgin will get pregnant. She'll bear a son and name him Immanuel."[4] Elizabeth knew Mary was the virgin Isaiah spoke of.

She stepped back and smiled warmly into Mary's eyes, cherishing their friendship. *We walk not by sight, but by faith, one moment at a time,* she thought. *And all the pieces of the puzzle are in place for me to understand this moment of truth. God knew the plan of my life from the beginning! My son John is to be the forerunner of the Messiah.*

The fulfilled promise of a Savior was Elizabeth's reward for her blameless character and her vital relationship with God.

---

[1] Luke 1:13–15, *The Message.*
 The name *Zachariah* was changed to conform to more traditional spelling.
[2] Genesis 17:17,19, *The Message.*
[3] Luke 1:42, *The Message.*
[4] Isaiah 7:14, *The Message.*

EMBRACING THE PENTECOSTAL PERSPECTIVE
What is the Holy Spirit teaching me?

Do you ever envy Bible personalities in whom God showed great trust? When you read Paul's and Elizabeth's stories, do you wonder if God would trust you with such important ministries? Before the downward spiral of comparison plunges you into the pit of self-pity, allow the Holy Spirit to remind you that God *does* place great trust in every person who chooses to access a saving relationship with Him through Jesus Christ.

God trusts us with divine transformation. Entering into a relationship with the Lord means stepping into a continuous cycle of change and growth. Paul went from persecutor to preacher. Elizabeth went from being barren to becoming the mother of the Savior's forerunner. And these are just two of the many changes they experienced in their relationships with God.

What do you see in Paul's relationship with God that you would like to see more of in your own relationship with Him?

What do you admire in Elizabeth's response to Zechariah's news and the subsequent events?

How do you need God to transform you so you will be more effective in your witness for Him?

God trusts us with great gifts. We're not talking about material gifts here. God gives incredible things like His Word, the gospel, power, love, self-discipline. When a child receives a gift from her parent, she then turns to that parent for help in its use. The intimacy of this relationship is enhanced by the gift-giving.

What gifts has God given you? Are you involving Him in their use?

How are you using God's gifts of power, love, and self-discipline?

God trusts us to rely on the Spirit. God is not an absentee Father trying to buy the affections of His children with costly presents. Rather, in His great love the Father sent the Holy Spirit to help us steward the precious life, calling, and gifts given. We are urged to guard—with the help of the Spirit—what He has entrusted to us.

Describe the actions you would take to guard your family in the face of threat.

Compare your answer above with how you are guarding your relationship with God and the trust He has placed in you.

How should you involve the Holy Spirit in your defense plan?

INVITING GOD TO CHANGE MY VIEW
What change is God asking me to make?

A relationship can be frighteningly fragile or incredibly enduring. The difference is your decision, or more correctly, it is a *series* of your decisions. Will you choose to give the time needed to nurture the relationship? Will you value the good in the relationship over and above the pain and difficulty of it? Will you allow relationships to invade your agenda?

One Saturday afternoon, I had crafted the perfect plan of action to complete my necessary work. The schedule was holding beautifully—until the phone began to ring. After eighty minutes spent with a friend going through a hard time, followed by fifteen minutes spent with a close friend, and then twenty minutes with a relative, my original plan was in shreds. I had a choice to make the instant I picked up the first call and at every point thereafter: withhold the time and attention each relationship needed in favor of my own interests or see the interruptions as opportunities to invest in people I value immensely. Simply articulating the choice makes the decision obvious.

Are you giving God enough of your time to build a strong relationship? Have you invited Him to be your Lord and Savior? Do you talk to Him continuously? Do you allow God to interrupt your agenda? Do you encourage it? How do you express to God how much you cherish your relationship with Him? What specifically would you like to improve in your relationship with the Lord?

Prayer

Heavenly Father, I thank You for planning our relationship from the very beginning of time. Though I can hardly comprehend the scope of Your love for me, I am dazzled by the lengths to which You have gone to make it possible. For transformation, gifts, and trust that elevate me to greater purpose, I thank You. Help me to show You every day how much I truly value knowing and walking with You. Stop me from ignoring You in favor of busyness, others, or some lesser thing. Enable me, through Your Spirit, to guard as precious the life that comes through Your Son, Jesus. Amen.

Journaling

Take a few minutes to record your personal insights from the lesson.

Her Relationship with Her Family

CATCHING SIGHT
Introduction

WE ARE WHO we are today because of those who have touched our lives in one way or another. One meaning of the word *touch* is "to leave a mark or impression upon." Think about how many different kinds of touch there are. There's touch that's not so nice, such as hitting or pinching. Then there's the playful touch, like tickling. There's loving touch—a squeeze of the hand, a pat on the arm, or a hug. In all of these examples, words aren't needed to get the point across. However, we know words can leave a mark or impression upon us. Words can uplift or words can hurt.

Your "touch" on the lives of your children, your spouse, your friends, and your coworkers is profound indeed. The imprints that shape us and ultimately help shape others around us are making their mark every day, whether we like it or not.

Have you ever noticed that Dad can have a bad day and if everyone just stays out of his way, they can make it through? However, if Mom has a bad day, everyone has a bad day! Have you also noticed with your children that you can do ninety-nine things right, but your child will copy the one not-so-good thing you did?

Our touch—our relationship with someone—does make a difference.

GETTING FOCUSED
Begin your study by considering the following:

Name some ways you can influence your family to serve God.

BIBLE READING
2 Timothy 1:4,5; Titus 2:3–5

New International Version

4 Recalling your tears, I long to see you, so that I may be filled with joy. 5 I have been reminded of your sincere faith, which first lived in your grandmother Lois and in your mother Eunice and, I am persuaded, now lives in you also.

Titus 2:3 Likewise, teach the older women to be reverent in the way they live, not to be slanderers or addicted to much wine, but to teach what is good. 4 Then they can train the younger women to love their husbands and children, 5 to be self-controlled and pure, to be busy at home, to be kind, and to be subject to their husbands, so that no one will malign the word of God.

New Living Translation

4 I long to see you again, for I remember your tears as we parted. And I will be filled with joy when we are together again. 5 I know that you sincerely trust the Lord, for you have the faith of your mother, Eunice, and your grandmother, Lois.

Titus 2:3 Similarly, teach the older women to live in a way that is appropriate for someone serving the Lord. They must not go around speaking evil of others and must not be heavy drinkers. Instead, they should teach others what is good. 4 These older women must train the younger women to love their husbands and their children, 5 to live wisely and be pure, to take care of their homes, to do good, and to be submissive to their husbands. Then they will not bring shame on the word of God.

GAINING BIBLICAL INSIGHT
Influencing my family to serve God

The scriptural model of family has its roots in God's command to Adam and Eve in Genesis 2:24. Here, God declares a man will leave his father and mother (his birth family) to join his wife in a marriage union, creating another family. It is the oldest social institution in existence, sometimes referred to as the basic cell of human social structure. Like a human body, society as a whole is healthy when the individual cells are healthy.

Throughout Scripture, we see this family pattern continuing. Sometimes the term *family* refers to the nuclear family of husband, wife, and their dependent children. Sometimes it refers to the extended family, including grandparents, grandchildren, uncles, aunts, and cousins. The biblical model of family has been the traditional model for many cultures throughout history.

Family relationships provide an important metaphor throughout Scripture. When Jesus began teaching about human relationship to deity, He described it as that of a son to a father. He taught His disciples to address God as "Father" when praying. In writing to the Ephesian church, Paul compares the relationship of Christ to the Church with that of a husband and wife. He uses another family metaphor when he addresses Timothy as his "son in the faith" (1 Timothy 1:2). A healthy view of family relationships strengthens our understanding of these scriptural metaphors.

The Family: Where Faith Is Communicated

When the aged Paul wrote to Timothy, he credited Timothy's birth family when he commended Timothy for his faith. In this family, faith was communicated to Timothy by his mother, Eunice, and grandmother, Lois. What a great gift for parents and grandparents to impart to their children!

Read 2 Timothy 1:3–6. How does Paul describe Timothy's faith?

The two words he used give us insight into the faith of Timothy's mother and grandmother. Apparently there was no discrepancy between the way these women lived and what they taught Timothy. Paul described their faith as "sincere." Their experience with the Lord had a ring of authenticity to it that reproduced itself in young Timothy.

Timothy's faith is also described by Paul as a "living" faith—the same kind of faith that "lived" in his mother and grandmother. His experience with the Lord was not just a theory, but an actuality. It was not a ritual he performed at certain times, but a reality that affected his entire life.

The context of daily family living provides one of the greatest opportunities to communicate the faith, and also one of the greatest challenges. Children who worship with their parents at church must also see the reality of their parents' experience in everyday life.

What are some of the ways parents can communicate a sincere, living faith at home?

The Family: Where Faith Is Demonstrated

Paul was more specific about communicating faith in his epistle to Titus. Here, he described the responsibilities of both the older and younger generations.

THE GRANDMOTHER'S FAITH

Grandparents have a significant role in the extended family. They no longer have direct responsibility for raising children, but they may still exert a powerful influence on the next generation. Paul gave instructions to Titus regarding what to teach people in cross-generational relationships.

List the instructions Paul gave to the older generation of women in Titus 2:3.

The grandparent generation serves as a role model, teaching by lifestyle as much as by words. A reverent, God-fearing life, including consistent words and actions, speaks volumes to the next generation. Consistency in Christian living testifies to God's faithfulness throughout life. The value of this kind of role model should never be underestimated, whether by children, grandchildren, or grandparents themselves. Those who do not have children or grandchildren of their own may still be role models, influencing children within the Christian community.

THE MOTHER'S FAITH

By comparison, how did Paul say the younger generation of women should live (Titus 2:4,5)?

Again, Paul's emphasis was on attitudes more than actions. Younger women should also demonstrate the love of God within the family context. Many women who are multitasking in family management easily understand the diligence he suggested. He exhorted them to show kindness in all things to bring honor to God and His Word.

Timothy's mother, Eunice, had the additional challenge of a cross-cultural marriage. According to Acts 16:1, Timothy's father was Greek. His mother, Eunice, was a Jewish Christian. These opposing ideologies had the potential to bring pressures into Timothy's home. But Paul described Eunice as a woman of living faith, which implies she not only believed in Christ, but she also lived an exemplary life in spite of these circumstances.

The Family: Where Faith Is Instilled

Training boys in the Hebrew Scriptures was a vital part of Jewish education. Typically, the formal training began at age five but it was normal to begin at-home training even before the child could speak.

The living faith Lois and Eunice imparted to Timothy was vitally rooted in the Word of God they taught in the home.

Today, the biblical training of children is often left to the church's Christian education ministries. Parents take their children to Sunday School and other Christian education activities to be trained in the Scriptures. This is a good practice, but it must be considered supplemental to training received in the home, and not a substitute.

List some possible ways to train children in the Scriptures at home.

Lois and Eunice are good role models. Let's look in on them now.

REFLECTING HIS IMAGE
Lois and Eunice (2 Timothy 1:5)

Humble hands that earlier held the small boy now placed him in his bed. Pulling the blanket tightly around him, her eyes moistened. Someday, she knew, she would shred the frayed blanket into rags without thinking twice about it, but not today. "Sleep well, my grandson," Lois whispered.

She slipped closer to the fireplace where her daughter, Eunice, was kneading bread for tomorrow's meal.

"Has his fever broken?" Eunice asked.

"Finally," Lois sighed. "Let's continue to pray he sleeps through the night. He asked countless 'What's that?' and 'Why?' questions today. He needs to rest, but he's definitely on the mend."

Together, mother and grandmother poured their lives and faith into small Timothy. He was the dearest thing in the world to them.

Life for the two women had not been easy. While being part of Greek culture had its advantages—masterful art, literature, and philosophy—Lois was a fervent Jewish Christian and lived her faith in all areas of her life. Because of this, she was seen as an outcast in her hometown, Lystra. Her faith was so obvious and firm that her daughter, Eunice, also became a Christian and lived a life devoted to Jesus.[1]

"Timothy will know the Holy Scriptures, because he knows *us*," Lois said on the day he was born. "We will not only talk about them, we will *live* them out as he grows from a boy to a man. From the fireplace where we prepare our meals to his bedside where we talk and pray, our faith will shine brightly enough to touch his life and bring him firmly into the family of God."

Lois and Eunice were committed women who lived their faith as they said they would. As Timothy's caregivers, they loved, disciplined, and taught him.

"Timothy," Eunice said one day at mealtime, "If Jesus were sitting here at the table with us, He would have admired your kindness, your warm smile, and your willingness to help others. Did you know when Jesus walked the earth, He loved to gather boys and girls around Him? He'd have them come up close and crowd around, and He'd listen to those boys and girls tell Him all about the things they really liked to do. Think of it, Timothy. He held boys just like you on His lap. Jesus looked into their eyes and He let them know how special they were."

I will always remember this moment, Eunice thought, choking back tears. *My son will leave home someday and, before I know it, he will find his own place in this world.* Embracing her young son, she whispered softly, "Jesus loves children, Timothy, and He loves you!"

Years passed and, as he grew to manhood, Timothy saw faith through the example of his grandmother and his mother. Through their actions and choices, he learned what it means to believe in God.

A weary Lois came through the door, breathing heavily from the long walk home from the village. "Eunice," she said, "I heard the most amazing thing today in the marketplace."

"Tell me," Eunice replied. "Have you heard news of Timothy?"

Smiling broadly, Lois said, "Some are saying my grandson may become another leader of the Church, just like Paul. And Paul's letters commend his faithful ministry."

That evening, Lois made her way to the worn wooden trunk. It was there somewhere. Slowly, almost ceremoniously, she lifted the tattered yellow blanket from the trunk. Holding it closely to her, she bowed her head and prayed. *Thank you, God, for the hope and assurance that we can trust You. As we water ministry to our family in prayer, You will see to it that the faith planted in our children's hearts will flower one day.*

---

[1] Jean E. Syswerda, ed., *Women of Faith Study Bible*, New International Version (Grand Rapids: Zondervan Corporation, 2001), 2080.

EMBRACING THE PENTECOSTAL PERSPECTIVE
What is the Holy Spirit teaching me?

The tender scene you just read may or may not reflect the environment in which you were raised. Lois and Eunice may be synonyms for your own family figures or merely another set of personalities, like those you read about in books or see in movies. In either case, you need to be able to translate God's ways into your present reality. His love covers a multitude of sins, and if you seek His help, you will find the grace to heal from past wounds and imitate His behavior.

Is it difficult for you to relate to God as your Father? Why or why not?

Describe your ideal of a Christian mother. Is this realistic or not?

What would you most like to be able to give to your family that you have not yet been able to emotionally and spiritually?

The day she received her learner's permit, a fifteen-year-old girl asked her parents if she could drive to church that evening. They denied her request explaining that she would need to begin by driving on the rural roads around their home. The girl asked, "Why?" She then added, "What's a rural road?" (Is it any wonder teenagers' insurance is so high?)

If you don't even know *what*—let alone *where*—the road is, how will you navigate it successfully? As a parent and a more mature believer in Christ, you have an enormous responsibility to guide your family and friends in their spiritual journey. Thankfully, this great responsibility is matched by great influence. More than any other person in the world, you have the power to influence positive change in their lives. Using this power wisely will require serious dependence on the Holy Spirit.

What do you need to be able to share the gospel with your unsaved family members? (e.g., the words to say, the courage to speak, the opportunity to share, the restoration of relationship, a life that matches the message)

What do you want your family to know about Jesus?

Families are under attack every day. As a God-ordained entity, the family constitutes a divine creation. Strong families bring health and strength to a society. Weak and broken families give the enemy easier access to wreak havoc. A unified, Spirit-filled defense, much like the one Lois and Eunice formed around Timothy, provides an essential component to the strength of your influence.

How do you apologize to your family members when you have said something hurtful?

What evidence of spiritual warfare do you recognize in your community? What is the greatest threat to your family?

What weapon do you need to sharpen to be better equipped for spiritual warfare on behalf of your family—prayer life in general, prayer in the Spirit, discernment, uncompromising faith, or something else?

How can you encourage other families to take up the shield of faith in a more intentional way?

INVITING GOD TO CHANGE MY VIEW

What change is God asking me to make?

In the mid-1800s, the northeastern United States was shaken by the ministry of evangelist Charles Finney. As a young adult, this lawyer met the Lord and experienced a mighty baptism in the Spirit. His prayer life and preaching were so powerfully anointed that sometimes people would literally fall under conviction of their sin as he entered a room. Thousands were saved and mobilized for service under his ministry.

A young woman once shared that her primary goal in life was to raise more "Finneys" for the kingdom of God. She was a very capable woman, who could have chosen from a number of ministry options, but she recognized the high calling of raising children who would dedicate themselves to God wholeheartedly. Though single and without children at the time, she embraced the idea of influencing her future family to serve God.

Do you understand the incredible influence you have as a wife, mother, sister, daughter, aunt, or grandmother? Ask the Lord to help you steward well this great influence. Petition Him for grace to be not just a good example, but a catalyst for growth in Christ. Do you have a family relationship for which you need healing before you can minister effectively? Will you allow the Holy Spirit to give you courage to speak boldly and lovingly with your family about their relationships with the Lord?

Prayer

Precious Savior, thank You for welcoming me into God's family. Through You, I know the power of divine grace and perfect love. Help me reflect those bountiful gifts to my family. Give me ears that always listen, words that always build up, and eyes to see each one as You do. In Your name I pray. Amen.

JOURNALING

Take a few minutes to record your personal insights from the lesson.

Her Relationship with Nonbelievers

CATCHING SIGHT

Introduction

ROGER STORMS, PASTOR of First Christian Church in Chandler, Arizona, tells this story:

"One Sunday, a car broke down in the alley behind our church, and the driver had jacked up the car and crawled underneath to work on the problem. Suddenly, we heard screams for help. The jack had slipped, and the car had come down on top of the man.

"Someone shouted, 'Call 911!' and a couple of people ran for the phone. Several of the men gathered around the large car and strained to lift it off the trapped man. Nurses from the congregation were rounded up and brought to the scene. Somehow, the men were able to ease the car's weight off the man, and he was pulled free. The nurses checked him over. He was scratched up and shaken, but otherwise OK."[1]

When this man was in peril, people did all they could to help—risking and inconveniencing themselves. Whatever was necessary to save this man, they were ready to try. We need this same attitude to rescue those in greatest peril—the danger of losing eternal life!

Often we look around us at our messed-up world and we wonder if we can really make a difference.

An old man, walking on the beach at dawn, noticed a young man ahead of him picking up starfish and flinging them into the sea. Catching up with the youth, the older man asked what he was doing. The

---

[1] Craig Brian Larson, ed., *Illustrations for Preaching and Teaching: From Leadership Journal* (Grand Rapids: Baker Books, 1993), 70.

33

answer was the stranded starfish would die if left in the morning sun.

"But the beach goes on for miles, and there are millions of starfish," countered the old man. "How can your effort make a difference?"

The young man looked at the starfish in his hand and then threw it to safety in the waves. "It makes a difference to this one," he said.

GETTING FOCUSED

Begin your study by considering the following:

The Bible describes two types of relationships: vertical and horizontal. Our primary relationship is with God—all other relationships flow out from it. Are there nonbelievers in your sphere of influence? Are you intentional about developing relationships with nonbelievers?

BIBLE READING

2 Timothy 1:5–12

New International Version

5 I have been reminded of your sincere faith, which first lived in your grandmother Lois and in your mother Eunice and, I am persuaded, now lives in you. 6 For this reason I remind you to fan into flame the gift of god, which is in you through the laying on of my hands. 7 For God did not give us a spirit of timidity, but a spirit of power, of love and of self-discipline.

8 So do not be ashamed to testify about our Lord, or ashamed of me his prisoner. But join with me in suffering for the gospel, by the power of God, 9 who has saved us and called us to a holy life—not because of anything we have done but because of his own purpose and grace. This grace was given us in Christ Jesus

New Living Translation

5 I know that you sincerely trust the Lord, for you have the faith of your mother, Eunice, and your grandmother, Lois. 6 This is why I remind you to fan into flames the spiritual gifts God gave you when I laid my hands on you. 7 For God has not given us a spirit of fear and timidity, but of power, love, and self-discipline. 8 So you must never be ashamed to tell others about our Lord. And don't be ashamed of me, either, even though I'm in prison for Christ. With the strength God gives you, be ready to suffer with me for the proclamation of the Good News.

9 It is God who saved us and chose us to live a holy life. He did this not because we deserved it, but because that was his plan long before the

New International Version

before the beginning of time, 10 but it has now been revealed through the appearing of our Savior, Christ Jesus, who has destroyed death and has brought life and immortality to light through the gospel. 11 And of this gospel I was appointed a herald and an apostle and a teacher. 12 That is why I am suffering as I am. Yet I am not ashamed, because I know whom I have believed, and am convinced that he is able to guard what I have entrusted to him for that day.

New Living Translation

world began—to show his love and kindness to us through Christ Jesus. 10 And now he has made all of this plain to us by the coming of Christ Jesus, our Savior, who broke the power of death and showed us the way to everlasting life through the Good News. 11 And God chose me to be a preacher, an apostle, and a teacher of this Good News.

12 And that is why I am suffering here in prison. But I am not ashamed of it, for I know the one in whom I trust, and I am sure that he is able to guard what I have entrusted to him until the day of his return.

GAINING BIBLICAL INSIGHT
Sharing my Savior with others

The thrust of Paul's ministry was the proclamation of the gospel. He radically committed himself to Jesus' command to preach the gospel to the entire world. Wherever Paul went, he told of Jesus' death, burial, and resurrection which constitute the very heart of the gospel. It is not surprising, then, to see him encouraging Timothy to make that same commitment.

Committed to Sharing the Gospel

Read 2 Timothy 1:7,8. Paul encouraged Timothy to be bold in sharing the gospel. Some think Timothy may have been timid, which might have kept him from easily sharing his faith. Some of us who have this temperament can understand his reticence. We can learn from what Paul taught Timothy.

Paul encouraged Timothy to remember some things for help in witnessing. Timothy had traveled with Paul on his second missionary journey and he could remember Paul's prayers. Paul reminded him that some of those prayers were for him. What great strength we can draw from being supported by friends in prayer!

Paul encouraged Timothy to remember his heritage of faith from his mother and grandmother. He also reminded him of the spiritual gifts he had received from the Father, gifts that should preclude fear when sharing his testimony.

From what Scripture says about Timothy, we know he was a committed young man living an exemplary Christian life, a necessary prerequisite for sharing faith. But Paul encourages him to be intentional in witnessing about the Lord, an act that might require boldness. While it is extremely important for our manner of living to show the love of Christ, it is equally important for us to share our faith verbally with others.

If you were Timothy, how would you have opened a conversation with an unbeliever with whom you wanted to share the gospel?

Paul thought perhaps Timothy would be ashamed of the gospel or ashamed of him because he was a prisoner. Timothy might have had a problem identifying with Paul if he had focused on Paul's circumstances. However, Paul tried to direct Timothy's thinking beyond the current situation to see the big picture and reminded him God had a purpose for the suffering.

Convinced of the Power of the Gospel

To be effective witnesses, we must be convinced of the power of the gospel to change lives. This awareness of God's power and presence was what kept Paul during his prison experience. Read verses 9 and 10 where, once again, Paul rehearses what the gospel can do for us.

What effect does the gospel have on a past sinful life?

To what kind of life does the gospel call us to live in the present?

What future hope do we have because of the work of Christ (which is the heart of the gospel)?

Timothy knew these truths about the gospel. He had also experienced the work of Christ in his own life. This personal experience was what Paul wanted him to share. We may not be articulate in Bible doctrines, but if we know the power of Christ's saving grace in our own lives we have something to share with others.

Paul reminded Timothy our salvation is by grace alone and not any goodness on our part. This knowledge is important to remember as we share our faith because some people may think they have to be good enough to earn God's favor. No one is ever saved by their own good works, but by the amazing grace of God who reaches us in our sin.

Courageous through Suffering for the Gospel

We might think everyone would accept this good news, but they do not. Those who do not accept the gospel often persecute those who do. Paul was experiencing that persecution as he wrote to Timothy from prison; yet suffering did not deter him from sharing the gospel.

As you read verses 11 and 12, observe Paul's attitude toward suffering. Note that suffering did not make him question his calling. He was assured of his calling as an apostle and teacher of the gospel in spite of what happened to him. Paul could be courageous in suffering because he was assured that his calling was from God.

Sometimes we are rebuffed or rejected when we try to witness. Our culture sometimes marginalizes us because we are Christians. In some areas of the world, people are being imprisoned for sharing the gospel today. When these things happen, it is easy to begin questioning God instead of following Paul's example of showing courage in suffering.

Paul had a deep confidence in God's power through difficulties. He strongly affirms his faith in verse 12. This is a good verse for every Christian to memorize because it gives insight into the source of Paul's confidence.

"I know whom I have believed," he stated boldly. He did not just know about God; he knew Him in a personal relationship. Though his present circumstances were very unpleasant, Paul had the assurance of a future with the Lord. This hope gave him courage in spite of his present suffering. He continued to fulfill his calling to share the gospel with unbelievers whatever his circumstances.

John 4 gives a great example of sharing a personal testimony. Jesus stopped briefly at the well in Samaria where He met a woman drawing water at noon, not the usual time for this practice. In the conversation that followed, the woman came to recognize who He was and went immediately to share the good news with others. We can learn from her actions.

REFLECTING HIS IMAGE
Woman at the Well (John 4)

She woke midmorning. After washing her face, she got dressed and lugged the clay jar across the floor as quietly as she could without waking him. *This feels heavy even when it's empty,* she thought.

She hated that jar.

Glancing back over her shoulder, she studied the man's sleeping face. She walked over to him and gently put her hand on his shoulder.

"I'm leaving now," she spoke in a low voice. The man nodded mechanically and rolled over. The woman fought back tears as the same self-loathing, haunting thoughts she had learned to live with flooded her mind—again. *So, this is what I've become? So starved for love and meaning that I carry water for anyone who will have me?*

The familiar trudge to the well was warm and dusty and *timely*. She had come here early in the morning several times a week since she was a young girl. Getting water was poor women's work. And in happier times she looked forward to talking and laughing with friends in the cool of the morning. *But that was then,* she whispered to herself. *Before I became an outcast. It's noon. The sun is up. By now, the others should be gone. Please. Let them be gone.*

She spotted the Man sitting down at the well, but she ignored His presence. *He's a Jew. If I move swiftly and pretend He's not here, I can draw my water and be gone,* she thought.

"Would you give me a drink of water?" the Man asked. Startled, she turned around, straightened her back, and held the water jar close to her.

At first, she did not acknowledge His question. He had no right to speak to her, no right to ask her for a drink. But something inside her wanted to respond. Perhaps it was her anger at the racial prejudice she had suffered at the hands of Jews all her life.

She continued to draw water in silence, but finally, just before she placed the heavy jar on her head to begin her walk back home, she turned to face her questioner with a question of her own.

"Why are you, a Jew, asking me, a Samaritan woman, for a drink?" The sound of her own voice surprised her. Not exactly anger, not disgust, or sarcasm. But an unexpected challenge to this nameless Man who had the nerve to speak to her at a well.

"If you knew the generosity of God and who I am, you would be asking Me for a drink, and I would give you fresh, living water."

For the next several minutes, they talked together: a Jewish man and a Samaritan woman. They spoke of the well's depth and the water. They talked about family heritage and the ancestry they shared.

But this common woman began to wonder about such an uncommon Man. Without apology or invitation, He asked something He had no right to ask. He inquired about her husband.

She set the clay jar down on the side of the well. She needed to hide—hide from a question with such a long and disappointing answer. But there was no place to hide in the presence of His piercing gaze.

She looked away, as if answering a question He had not asked. "I have no husband," she said.

"That's nicely put: 'I have no husband.' You've had five husbands, and the man you're living with now isn't even your husband. You spoke the truth there, sure enough."

How can this Man know so much about me? she wondered. *He must be a prophet.*

She listened as He spoke of true and honest worship. She listened as He talked. He spoke of the importance of who you are and the way you live. He noticed her thirst. He acknowledged her hunger. But her longing would never be satisfied with bread and water.

"I am the Messiah you've been waiting for," said Jesus. "You don't have to wait any longer."

Suddenly an air of peace came over her and her eyes could see a future with hope. *Could this be the Messiah? Is He who He claims to be?* She believed Him. Standing there by that well, she became well. While she drew water, she came upon the Living Water. No more questions. No more discussion. She could not wait. She would not wait. She ran all the way back to Sychar to tell her story.

The woman whose guilt caused her to avoid others now sought them out. *Surely they'll believe me. I'm talking about the Christ, the Messiah! This is something real.*

"Look in His eyes," she exclaimed to the townspeople as she described Jesus. "See His compassion. Come see this Man."

It was not until the next day, really, that she missed it. She remembered the jar. With a certain lightness in her step, she made her way back to the well, back to where she was just yesterday. And there, she found the jar. Empty. Isolated. And off to the side of the well. She smiled as her hands lifted the clay vessel. Lighter now. The jar was not as heavy as she remembered. And filling it was not the burdensome chore it had been the day before, either.

As she began filling the jar, the sound of the pouring water caused her to be aware of something totally new for her: She wasn't hungry. She wasn't thirsty. And because of her testimony, many others met this Man, Jesus, just as she had met Him—through an extraordinary encounter.

Lifting the water to her shoulder, she began her walk home.

She loved that clay jar.

EMBRACING THE PENTECOSTAL PERSPECTIVE
What is the Holy Spirit teaching me?

We may not know her name, but we love her story! The woman at the well illustrates beautiful "before" and "after" pictures of life in Christ. Her thirst for life, wonder about the Savior, impatience for His appearing, and immediate evangelism illustrate the very essence of Christian witness.

Today, we need to operate from the same basic values in order to influence the lives of people around us. Nothing beats knowing Jesus, so how could we withhold that precious knowledge from the people in our lives? Just as we are dependent upon the Spirit to lead us to Christ, we must rely on Him to lead us to others who need the Lord.

Do you believe Jesus is the only way to be saved?

Have you shared a verbal witness of the gospel with someone in the last thirty days? If not, why not?

Name three people in your circle of influence who need Jesus—one family member, one coworker, friend, or neighbor, and one fringe acquaintance (e.g., parent of a child in your child's class, attendant at your gym, librarian).

Paul reminded Timothy that the Lord saves us and calls us to a holy life (2 Timothy 1:9). The holy life—imparted and nurtured by the Holy Spirit—includes living in a God-honoring manner and loving with a God-sized capacity. We will never accomplish either in our own strength, but by yielding our lives to the Spirit, we can demonstrate the gospel with our words and actions. Remember, most people come to Jesus through a personal relationship with another Christian. *You* may be the best hope of salvation for the people in your world.

How should you pray for people who need Jesus? Are you doing it?

How can you strengthen relationships to create credible and comfortable opportunities for talking about the Lord?

What do you need to repent of in order to create space in your heart for more of God's love for people?

Boredom, for too many reasons to mention, should be considered sin to the believer. Picture the woman at the well charging into town, shouting to everyone she meets. Envision Timothy meeting the challenges of his growing new church. Does either one strike you as complacent? No! God's people have access to too much to grow accustomed to their surroundings. Chief among the wonderful resources provided to the Christian is great power for witness through the Holy Spirit. Exhilaration is far too tame a word to describe the experience of leading someone to the Lord. Risk losing your fear and lack of confidence in order to gain unspeakable joy and another brother or sister in Christ!

What does a person need to know or do to be saved?

What are you afraid of when it comes to sharing the gospel?

What do you need to be more effective in sharing the gospel?

INVITING GOD TO CHANGE MY VIEW
What change is God asking me to make?

An old Christian song expressed the desire to have the "Father's eyes"—the ability to see people as our Heavenly Father does. A newer chorus prays, "Open the eyes of my heart, Lord," with a focus on seeing the Lord in the fullness of His glory. Both create the bifocal prescription necessary for effective witness. We will not be compelled to share a Savior whose greatness we do not appreciate, nor will we have the compassion to share with a person when we do not care enough to look past the outer layer.

The testimony of the woman at the well carries a wonderful example for every believer. Her desire, wonder, and unstoppable need to share the good news with others inspire us to do the same. But we should also look to the Lord's example. He had the heart and audacity to sit by a well in a region normally avoided, at a time usually devoid of activity, to speak to a woman overlooked by society.

Do you need to see people with the vision of Jesus? Do you need a heart of compassion? Will you confess your hardheartedness toward people outside of the family of Christ?

Will you ask the Lord for divine appointments with people who need to know Him? Will you pray for boldness to witness?

Prayer

Jesus, I am not ashamed of You. I want to lead others to You. Enable me to see people like You do—people who cross my path every day and people off the beaten path. Fill me with the love and boldness of Your Spirit. Give me souls, Lord. For your sake, Amen.

JOURNALING

Take a few minutes to record your personal insights from the lesson.

Her Relationship with Believers

CATCHING SIGHT
Introduction

M Y MOTHER, GRANDMOTHER, and I had been talking as we shopped for fabric when we realized it was lunchtime. The stranger browsing next to us was alone, so my grandmother didn't miss a beat when she said, "I see you are alone. Would you like to join us for lunch?" The stranger did, and for the next thirty years, my grand-mother and this woman shared a close friendship.

Our last lesson was on building relationships with nonbelievers in order to influence them for the Kingdom. This lesson deals with our relationships with believers. Through small group activities and church social events, we certainly have many opportunities to develop friendships within the Christian community.

Friendship in today's world is a special gift. Friendships are not all alike, just as friends are not all alike. Some we can relax with; others revive us with new thoughts. Some people hold friendships through a lifetime of experiences, while others become friends with one uniquely shared experience. Sometimes we work at being friends, and sometimes friendships "just happen." Each friendship is as varied and interesting as the two people who make up the relationship.

People are not made to have intimate friendships with a large number of others. Women value friendships and guard them carefully. Sometimes we choose a friend based on our own needs, sometimes we choose friendship based on the needs we see we can meet in someone else. Emilie Barnes and Donna Otto, in *Friends of the Heart,* say, "Choosing friends, then, is a part of knowing ourselves, realizing that certain associations strengthen us, teach us, and fill our needs, while others push our buttons or feed our weaknesses."[1] Barnes and Otto also say, "We love the picture painted in the Book of Ecclesiastes: 'A threefold cord is not quickly broken' (4:12). To us, that is a picture of the two of us entwined in a friendship that includes God as a third member. It's like silken cords girded with steel. We trust it. We cherish it."[2]

GETTING FOCUSED

Begin your study by considering the following:

One of Robert Schuller's prayers reads, "Lord, there are some people who, when I am around them, fatigue me. And there are other people who, surrounding me, energize me. Jesus, you are that exciting kind of person! I draw so much energy-producing enthusiasm for living when I allow Your Spirit to fill my life."[3] What kind of a friend are you?

[1] Emilie Barnes and Donna Otto, *Friends of the Heart* (Eugene, Ore.: Harvest House Publishers, 1999), 49.

[2] Ibid., 73.

[3] Robert H. Schuller, *Positive Prayers for Power-Filled Living* (New York: Bantam Books, 1997), 29.

BIBLE READING

Proverbs 17:17; 18:24; 27:9; Ecclesiastes 4:10; 2 Timothy 1:16–18

New International Version	*New Living Translation*
Proverbs 17:17 A friend loves at all times, and a brother is born for adversity.	Proverbs 17:17 A friend is always loyal, and a brother is born to help in time of need.
18:24 A man of many companions may come to ruin, but there is a friend who sticks closer than a brother.	8:24 There are "friends" who destroy each other, but a real friend sticks closer than a brother.
27:9 Perfume and incense bring joy to the heart, and the pleasantness of one's friend springs from his earnest counsel.	27:9 The heartfelt counsel of a friend is as sweet as perfume and incense.
Ecclesiastes 4:10 If one falls down,	Ecclesiastes 4:10 If one person falls, the other can reach out and help. But people who are alone when they

New International Version

his friend can help him up. But pity the man who falls and has no one to help him up!

2 Timothy 1:16 May the Lord show mercy to the household of Onesiphorus, because he often refreshed me and was not ashamed of my chains. 17 On the contrary, when he was in Rome, he searched hard for me until he found me. 18 May the Lord grant that he will find mercy from the Lord on that day! You know very well in how many ways he helped me in Ephesus.

New Living Translation

fall are in real trouble.

2 Timothy 1:16 May the Lord show special kindness to Onesiphorus and all his family because he often visited and encouraged me. He was never ashamed of me because I was in prison. 17 When he came to Rome, he searched everywhere until he found me. 18 May the Lord show him special kindness on the day of Christ's return. And you know how much he helped me at Ephesus.

GAINING BIBLICAL INSIGHT
Encouraging my Christian friends to thrive

On the Day of Pentecost, many people became believers in Christ. In the days that followed, they were drawn together for prayer and fellowship. It soon became evident a new community was being formed—a community of people who became known as "Christians."

The English language does not have an exact word for the relationship of people within this community. They are not biologically related as family, yet the relationship feels like that found within a loving family. They are friends in the usual meaning of friendship, but the relationship is deeper. Most friendships are based on commonalities, but in the Christian community, people of different backgrounds, personalities, and socioeconomic status come together. Their only commonality may be their relationship to Christ, yet they relate deeply to one another.

Much of the New Testament gives instructions for relating within the Christian community. Paul concluded many of his epistles with warm greetings to his friends. He wrote to Timothy about his relationship with Onesiphorus, giving an example of the way Christians can encourage each other in the faith.

Friendship That Refreshes

This letter was sent from a Roman prison to Timothy in Ephesus. The church in Ephesus began with an outpouring of the Holy Spirit (Acts 19). At the end of Paul's ministry, he bid a tearful farewell to the elders of the Ephesian church, telling them he would not see them again (Acts 20). In reading these passages, we sense the warmth of Paul's relationship to this church.

One man from Ephesus apparently had visited Paul in prison in Rome. Of this visit Paul states: "He [Onesiphorus] often refreshed me" (2 Timothy 1:16). What a great description of the effect one good friend can have upon another, particularly in distressing circumstances. The word *refresh* refers to the feeling one has after taking a cool drink on a very hot day. Paul had been "bearing the heat" of accusations and imprisonment. By his visit, Onesiphorus brought relief from that pressure.

Proverbs 27:9 compares this aspect of friendship to the fragrance of perfume. "Perfume and incense bring joy to the heart, and the pleasantness of one's friend springs from his earnest counsel."

What qualities in friendship bring this fragrant refreshing to you?

Some things to look for in friends are openness in conversation, an accepting, nonjudgmental attitude, and sincerity. You probably can think of other necessary characteristics. Whatever it looks like, friendship should always have the effect of encouraging others by refreshing their spirits.

Friendship That Is Loyal

Paul had lived earlier in his own rented house, even though he was a prisoner. Now he was confined to a dungeon, chained like a criminal. Onesiphorus could have been embarrassed to associate with Paul in these circumstances, but he was not ashamed of Paul's chains according to 2 Timothy 1:16.

Faithful friends are loyal, whatever the circumstances. Proverbs 17:17 states "A friend loves at all times, and a brother is born for adversity."

It is commonly said, "You can tell who your friends are when you are in trouble." Loyal friends stand by us in the tough times. Some hard times come that are not our own doing, such as disastrous storms, unavoidable accidents, and disease. All of us need loyal friends who will stand by us during these times, helping us according to our need.

What obstacles might someone have to overcome to remain loyal to a friend?

Sometimes we create our own difficulties through poor judgment and wrong choices. These times pose a real test for friendship, but a loyal friend stands by. If a friend loves "at all times" as Proverbs says, the friendship will survive even when we mess up our own lives.

Friendship That Is Devoted

Paul's friendship with Onesiphorus began in Ephesus. For reasons unknown to us, Onesiphorus made trips to Rome where he searched the many prisons until he found his friend, Paul. Apparently, Onesiphorus valued their friendship enough that he was willing to put forth the effort needed to find Paul.

Friendships may be lost when a determined effort is not made to maintain the relationship. We may not have friends who are physically imprisoned, but they have other needs. Devoted friends search all possibilities until they find the keys to minister to a friend's need.

Proverbs 18:24 tells us, "There is a friend who sticks closer than a brother." Onesiphorus was that kind of friend for Paul. Circumstances had separated them physically, but the bond of friendship held them together, enabling Onesiphorus to minister to Paul.

Friendship That Is Helpful

When Paul was in Ephesus, Onesiphorus helped in many ways according to 2 Timothy 1:18. What that help was, we do not know. He could have helped Paul by supplying his basic physical needs while in prison.

True friendship should be mutually supportive. "If one falls down, his friend can help him up. But pity the man who falls and has no one to help him up" (Ecclesiastes 4:10).

Friends help friends—whatever the need. This helpful spirit is a mark of true friendship. We know from Hebrews 6:10 that God regards helpfulness to others as evidence of love shown toward Him. This friendly relationship should mark the Christian community.

Paul names many friends in writing the Epistles. One was a woman named Phoebe, a friend he trusted to carry his epistle to the Roman church. This epistle became part of our sacred Scripture. Let's hear Paul's story of his friendship with Phoebe.

REFLECTING HIS IMAGE
Phoebe (Romans 16:1,2)

Dear Friends,

I first met Phoebe when I was a convert to Christianity and in trouble. Food was scarce, money was nonexistent, and the church in Cenchrea came to my rescue just when thoughts of fear, desperation, and discouragement crept in. I was a man on a mission—serving the spiritual needs of non-Jewish people so they could know Jesus Christ and be made whole by God's Holy Spirit. And I needed help!

The door opened before I could reach for it. Phoebe recognized me and her predictable reaction told me I was welcome. Her door creaked a song of welcome as I made my way into her house that day. Without ceremony, she bowed her head slightly and then looked straight into my face, smiling warmly.

"Welcome to my home, Paul," she said. "You are an honored guest." Her house smelled of citrus and antique tradition. As we sat down together, her small frame lost its definition in the yards of material in her plain dress.

No offense. No pretense. No guile. Just transparent humanity. I listened for the next hour or so to my new friend as she shared encouraging reports of accomplishments in the church. Quiet and direct and deep in the things of God.

You know, there are certain things to love about life—homemade bread, hot soup full of meat and vegetables, beautiful flower gardens. Phoebe knows a lot about the niceties of homemaking. On more than one occasion, she opened her home to me and my friends. But she also knows that, while these things have value, we won't take any of them to heaven with us. Only people go to heaven. As a deaconess in her church, she works for things eternal. Everything else is secondary.

I soon learned that Jesus is her model and she believes God intends for her to be His witness on earth.

Life has been richer for me these past months because of Phoebe praying for my ministry, hosting church in her home, teaching, caring for the poor. The list goes on and on.

While this letter is primarily about you who are believers in Rome, it also allows me to tell you about this amazing friend who has helped me in my ministry.

Be sure to welcome Phoebe with all the generous hospitality we Christians are famous for. I wholeheartedly endorse her and her work. She's a key representative in the church at Cenchrea. Help her in whatever way she asks. She deserves anything you can do for her. She's helped many people, including me.

Kind regards,
Paul

Like Phoebe, you may work for the Lord in relative obscurity, but your name is known where it matters, and the work you do makes a difference.[1]

---

[1] Jean E. Syswerda, ed., *Women of Faith Study Bible*, New International Version (Grand Rapids: Zondervan Corporation, 2001), 2048.

EMBRACING THE PENTECOSTAL PERSPECTIVE
What is the Holy Spirit teaching me?

"With friends like these, who needs enemies?" So goes a familiar phrase. It would have applied to the traitor Judas or the fair-weather Demas, but never to Phoebe, Onesiphorus, or Timothy. These people in Paul's life demonstrated great worth, and he honored them by counting them as his friends. Theirs were mutual relationships— giving and receiving. Can you match their résumés?

Phoebe could be trusted with serious responsibility. In what serious ways do you need to be found trustworthy to serve your friends well?

Onesiphorus visited his friend during a difficult time—not just on Day One of the trial, but well into it. How could you tangibly touch a friend's life this week who struggles with a long-held burden?

Timothy relied on Paul's counsel. Do you seek the wisdom of the Spirit before giving advice to your friends? How can you be more sensitive to the Spirit's leading when guiding friends?

Timothy and Phoebe had found Paul to be a good friend, one to be trusted. A friend proves herself in small and large things. Your friend tells you when you have lipstick on your teeth and whether your nose is "debris free." But she will also tell you when you are acting unwisely. While acquaintances flatter or unthinkingly agree, your friend speaks the truth in love—truth that is illuminated by God's Spirit.

Do you allow friends close enough to hold you accountable for your walk with Christ? If not, why not? If so, is that relationship growing deeper or staying the same?

Are you a friend who addresses or ignores the ugly stuff?

The Holy Spirit gives understanding, boldness, perseverance, prophetic words, and healing words. Which will help you most to be a better friend?

A friend's words of encouragement—spoken to us in just the right moment or spoken to our Heavenly Father on our behalf—compose one of the greatest gifts of friendship. Christian friends should be especially good at cheering and praying for one another. Without Paul's encouragement and intercession, it is not likely that either Timothy or Phoebe would have stepped into roles of leadership in the church, let alone succeeded as they did. Paul no doubt saw their potential before they recognized it in themselves. That's what friends do.

How can you become a world-class encourager?

How does praying in the Spirit for your friends make a difference in their lives and yours?

INVITING GOD TO CHANGE MY VIEW
What change is God asking me to make?

On a bright and sunny Florida morning, a crowd gathered near Cape Canaveral to watch the launch of a space shuttle. People were laughing, jostling one another, focusing on staking out their own territory, and generally oblivious to those around them. After the launch, however, the scene changed dramatically. Voices were hushed, actions courteous, and conversations crossed the groups' boundaries. It seemed the shared experience had united the strangers.

When Jesus was preparing to return to heaven, He assured His closest friends, the disciples, that He would not leave them alone. They would be accompanied by the Holy Spirit, the One who would walk alongside. "Sticking closer than a brother," which describes human friendship in Proverbs 18:24, fails to capture the fullness of the relationship possible with the Holy Spirit.

God sent His Holy Spirit to help us see Jesus in His awesome magnificence every day. When the community of Christ seeks the fullness of the Spirit, they experience a unity that defies attack. The Holy Spirit stays with us at all times and empowers us with the fruit necessary to build lasting relationships.

Have you invited Jesus Christ to be your Lord, your best Friend? Do you need to be filled with the Holy Spirit? Do you need to repair a relationship with a friend? Will you invite the Spirit to help you speak the truth in love to a friend? Would you like to ask God to bring more friends to your life?

Prayer

Father, my mind is still boggled by the fact that You call us Your friends. Friendship with You, my Holy God, is simultaneously terrifying and fascinating. Thank You for inviting me to be a part of a personal relationship, not an impersonal contract. I want to grow so close to You that I never fail to see Your glory. Let me share the graces of that friendship—love, faithfulness, encouragement, and hope—with my friends. Help me be a good friend, a best friend, to each of them and to You. Amen.

JOURNALING

Take a few minutes to record your personal insights from the lesson.

Her Relationship in Discipling

CATCHING SIGHT

Introduction

A TRUE DISCIPLER is one who not only tells others about Jesus, but spends time investing in their lives.

"You can't really help her," a young woman told me emphatically one day.

"Why not?" I asked, surprised.

"Because your parents weren't alcoholics, you didn't come from a dysfunctional family, you didn't attend Bible school, and you weren't sexually abused!" she declared.

"Are you saying I can help people only if I've had the same experiences they have?" I inquired.

"Exactly," she replied with great certainty.

The woman talking to me had been a great help to many people recovering from childhood trauma and would certainly be able to empathize, since she had suffered some of the same experiences in her past.

"Was Jesus the child of an alcoholic?" I asked her.

"That's different," she replied. "Jesus can help anyone because He is Jesus."

"Okay," I countered, "but when you're sick, you don't look for a doctor who's had all the diseases in the book, or a dentist who has false teeth, do you?"

"Of course not," she said defensively.

"The doctor knows his field well enough to diagnose your illness, refer you to an expert, or prescribe medicine," I said. "A Christian can't possibly match all of life's experiences, but we can become spiritually mature enough to have a wise word for a new believer, a wounded person, or an unsaved person. Above all, we can show people how to have a relationship with Jesus."

Believers should share their faith and become actively involved in discipling others, in and out of the church. Jesus' faithful disciples were ordinary men and women who became extraordinary because of Jesus Christ. You can do the same!

GETTING FOCUSED

Begin your study by considering the following:

Discuss ways people would change if they realized every encounter was an opportunity for discipleship.

BIBLE READING

2 Timothy 2:1–15; 4:1–5

New International Version	New Living Translation
1 You then, my son, be strong in the grace that is in Christ Jesus. 2 And the things you have heard me say in the presence of many witnesses entrust to reliable men who will also be qualified to teach others.	1 Timothy, my dear son, be strong with the special favor God gives you in Christ Jesus. 2 You have heard me teach many things that have been confirmed by many reliable witnesses. Teach these great truths to trustworthy people who are able to pass them on to others.
3 Endure hardship with us like a good soldier of Christ Jesus. 4 No one serving as a soldier gets involved in civilian affairs—he wants to please his commanding officer. 5 Similarly, if anyone competes as an athlete, he does not receive the victor's crown unless he competes according to the rules. 6 The hardworking farmer should be the first to receive a share of the crops. 7 Reflect on what I am saying, for the Lord will give you insight into all this.	3 Endure suffering along with me, as a good soldier of Christ Jesus. 4 And as Christ's soldier, do not let yourself become tied up in the affairs of this life, for then you cannot satisfy the one who has enlisted you in his army. 5 Follow the Lord's rules for doing his work, just as an athlete either follows the rules or is disqualified and wins no prize. 6 Hardworking farmers are the first to

New International Version

8 Remember Jesus Christ, raised from the dead, descended from David. This is my gospel, 9 for which I am suffering even to the point of being chained like a criminal. But God's word is not chained. 10 Therefore I endure everything for the sake of the elect, that they too may obtain the salvation that is in Christ Jesus, with eternal glory.

11 Here is a trustworthy saying: If we died with him, we will also live with him; 12 if we endure, we will also reign with him. If we disown him, he will also disown us; 13 if we are faithless, he will remain faithful, for he cannot disown himself.

14 Keep reminding them of these things. Warn them before God against quarreling about words; it is of no value, and only ruins those who listen. 15 Do your best to present yourself to God as one approved, a workman who does not need to be ashamed and who correctly handles the word of truth.

4:1 In the presence of God and of Christ Jesus, who will judge the living and the dead, and in view of his appearing and his kingdom, I give you this charge: 2 Preach the Word; be prepared in season and out of season; correct, rebuke and encourage—with great patience and careful instruction. 3 For the time will come when men will not put up with sound doctrine. Instead, to suit their own desires, they will gather around them a great

New Living Translation

enjoy the fruit of their labor. 7 Think about what I am saying. The Lord will give you understanding in all these things.

8 Never forget that Jesus Christ was a man born into King David's family and that he was raised from the dead. This is the Good News I preach. 9 And because I preach this Good News, I am suffering and have been chained like a criminal. But the word of God cannot be chained. 10 I am willing to endure anything if it will bring salvation and eternal glory in Christ Jesus to those God has chosen.

11 This is a true saying: If we die with him, we will also live with him. 12 If we endure hardship, we will reign with him. If we deny him, he will deny us. 13 If we are unfaithful, he remains faithful, for he cannot deny himself. 14 Remind everyone of these things, and command them in God's name to stop fighting over words. Such arguments are useless, and they can ruin those who hear them. 15 Work hard so God can approve you. Be a good worker, one who does not need to be ashamed and who correctly explains the word of truth.

4:1 And so I solemnly urge you before God and before Christ Jesus—who will someday judge the living and the dead when he appears to set up his Kingdom: 2 Preach the word of God. Be persistent, whether

New International Version

number of teachers to say what their itching ears want to hear. 4 They will turn their ears away from the truth and turn aside to myths. 5 But you, keep your head in all situations, endure hardship, do the work of an evangelist, discharge all the duties of your ministry.

New Living Translation

the time is favorable or not. Patiently correct, rebuke, and encourage your people with good teaching.

3 For a time is coming when people will no longer listen to right teaching. They will follow their own desires and will look for teachers who will tell them whatever they want to hear. 4 They will reject the truth and follow strange myths.

5 But you should keep a clear mind in every situation. Don't be afraid of suffering for the Lord. Work at bringing others to Christ. Complete the ministry God has given you.

GAINING BIBLICAL INSIGHT
Investing my faith in new believers

On Paul's second missionary journey, he met Timothy, a believer in Lystra. Seeing potential in the young man, Paul invited him to join his traveling group as they visited the churches in Asia. The relationship between the two became like that of father and son.

Second Timothy was the last letter from the aged Paul to his "son in the gospel." The opening verses reveal the closeness of their relationship. Paul wrote of his desire to see Timothy, told him about his prayers for him, and encouraged him in his ministry. By studying this relationship, we learn ways in which we can invest our faith in new believers.

The Grace that Brings the Gospel

Timothy was already a believer when he met Paul. In their travels together, he heard Paul preach many times about the saving grace of Jesus Christ. He probably would have read Paul's epistle to the Ephesians, in which Paul eloquently outlines salvation by grace: "For it is by grace you have been saved, through faith—and this not from yourselves, it is the gift of God—not by works, so that no one can boast" (2:8,9).

Then, the elderly Paul encouraged Timothy to "be strong in the grace that is in Christ Jesus" (2 Timothy 2:1). He did not want Timothy to get away from his spiritual roots, and reminded him salvation is by grace, not works. Paul also wanted Timothy to know the *saving* grace of Christ is also the *sustaining* grace that enables him to live the Christian life and fulfill his calling.

The Responsibility of Sharing the Gospel

Having established grace as the foundation for Timothy's life and ministry, Paul moved into the heart of the discipling relationship. He reminded Timothy of his responsibility to share the gospel with others: "The things you have heard me say in the presence of many witnesses entrust to reliable men who will also be qualified to teach others" (2:2).

This instruction is in direct obedience to the Great Commission, in which the Lord commanded His disciples to preach the gospel to the entire world. The monumental task of world evangelism is the responsibility of all believers. Every Christian can participate by using the simple method Paul described to Timothy: Share what you know about Christ with others, who will also do the same thing.

Sometimes the clarity of the gospel message is muddied by irrelevant side issues. Paul warned Timothy about this possibility, encouraging him to focus on the positive aspect of the message without becoming involved in meaningless arguments (2:14).

The Disciplined Life of the Person Sharing the Gospel

Paul wanted Timothy to know this life is not easy. He followed the instruction to "endure hardship" by referencing three lifestyles which require rigid personal discipline.

Read 2 Timothy 2:4–6. List qualities of personal discipline in the lives of the soldier, the athlete, and the farmer. Which of these qualities do you think a Christian should emulate when sharing the gospel?

Soldier:

Athlete:

Farmer:

For what reasons do each of these people live a disciplined lifestyle?

Paul told Timothy to reflect on what he was saying. We should do the same thing. **What do you think Paul's reason was for including these illustrations in his letter to Timothy?**

Paul knew Timothy would encounter difficult situations in sharing the gospel. He reminded him others endured hardship for different reasons. The gospel has eternal rewards, not only for Timothy, but also for those hearing the gospel from him. This perspective would minimize any hardship Timothy might endure.

The Solid Foundation for the Gospel

The gospel of grace Paul preached and Timothy experienced has its roots in the Word of God. As Paul sat in prison, bound in chains, his consolation was that God's Word was not chained. He instructed Timothy to reflect, or meditate, on the things he had written and to have others do the same thing. "Keep reminding them of these things," he told Timothy (2:14).

Remembering, meditating, reflecting—all these words refer to thought processes by which we may increase our understanding of the Word of God. When we *remember* God's Word, we are answering the question: "What does God's Word say?" When we *meditate* upon it, we answer the question: "What does God's Word mean?" When we *reflect* on its passages, we ask: "What does God's Word mean to me?" Together, these three processes give us a valuable method of hiding God's Word in our heart.

Paul also instructed Timothy to be a person who properly handles the word of truth (2:15).

How does one "correctly handle" the word of truth?

Every generation of Christians since Paul's time has been faced with this responsibility. God's Word has been passed from generation to generation, orally and in written form. In whatever manner the Word comes to us, we become responsible for properly handling it and passing it on. Ignoring or distorting its message demonstrates an inappropriate handling of the Word. The only correct response is to accept it, live by it, and pass its vital message on to others. This response is the heart of discipleship.

Part of the process of correctly handling the Word of God is sharing it with others. Paul challenged Timothy to "preach the Word" (4:2). Timothy shared God's Word through preaching. But there are many ways of sharing the Word as we verbalize our faith in daily conversation and live to demonstrate the reality of the Word.

Naomi was a woman who must have shared her faith in several distressing situations convincingly enough to influence her daughter-in-law Ruth to follow her to Bethlehem. Let's see what Naomi has to say.

REFLECTING HIS IMAGE
Naomi (Ruth 1)

The sun refused to shine the morning I buried my son. A cold, steady drizzle, mixed with salty tears, drenched my eyes and face. *I'm too weary to even talk. How can I find the strength to lift my head in the presence of my friends?* I asked myself. As I followed the funeral procession down that endless, muddy road, I felt numb and oblivious to everyone and everything around me. The wind howled like never before and I realized it wasn't just the winter gale causing me to shiver. I was afraid. In fact, I hit rock bottom. I could see no "great plan" of God working in my life. After losing my husband and both sons, I saw only heartache and struggle.

It all began when Elimelech gave up his inheritance in Judah during a famine and moved us to Moab to try to provide for our family. We had two boys, Mahlon and Kilion. Good boys, both of them, but I'll confess, their choices to marry Moabite women upset me. After all, it was against the law of Moses to marry pagan wives. It took me a while to accept them, but, as time passed, both women embraced our way of life and the God we serve and, eventually, we developed a deep love and respect for each other.

Orpah is the more outgoing of the two, talkative and logical, while Ruth is serene, yet well spoken. Two very different women, for sure. But together, along with my husband and sons, we were a family.

I observed the women many mornings as they went about their daily chores, especially Ruth. She never seemed to be in a great hurry. Instead, her steps were measured. No job she began was ever considered finished until it was absolutely perfect, whether it was preparing a loaf of fresh baked bread or scrubbing a dirty pot.

In the middle of long summer afternoons, we would go for walks. And we would talk—about God. I've always spoken easily about God, because He is real to me. I suppose Ruth's relationship with God began the way most do. She came to know and value someone who knows Him well. That person was me. A deep bond formed between us.

"God loves to walk alongside us, every day. He always has," I said to her on one of our outings. "Since the beginning, when He strolled the Garden with Adam and Eve, He has been interested in touching, talking to, and interacting with His creation. He's still interested. Take time to watch and listen, Ruth. You'll find God in ordinary ways and discover His extraordinary plans for the future."

Those words would swirl in my mind again and again over the next several months as the unthinkable happened. All three men in my household died, leaving my daughters-in-law and me destitute. Imagine: three women—helpless. No property, no money, no future. How was I to care for us with no means of support? Day after day, I fearfully cried out to God for help.

Finally, He answered. He seemed to be saying, "If you're going to be a follower, then follow Me."

Life in Moab—as I had known it—was over. The only answer for me was to go home, back to Judah, back to relatives who might agree to support me. I knew the days ahead would be long and treacherous. The last thing I needed was more responsibility! But Ruth and Orpah insisted on traveling with me.

On the road, I told both of them to go back home, back to their families where they would be cared for until they could marry again.

Orpah agreed, but I was not prepared for Ruth's response. I'll never forget the look in her eyes and the deep devotion to God that crept into her voice when she spoke.

"I am not naive, Naomi," she said. "I have faced rejection and in-dignation from my own people. I am aware of the resentment against me in Bethlehem. But I will never turn away from the love I have found in you. I will not let go of you or your God who is now my God too. Never."

As I embraced my daughters-in-law, my thoughts took me back to funeral processions and long, winding roads, and my eyes were washed with tears again—this time so I could more clearly see God's hand and handiwork in my own life.

The friendship Ruth and I shared as we journeyed on together helped pull us through the hardest of times and continued to teach us about the true importance of faith and families, and showing others how to follow God.

Don't be surprised about what God allows to come your way. Every day will have some living, some dying, and some living again.

EMBRACING THE PENTECOSTAL PERSPECTIVE
What is the Holy Spirit teaching me?

Ruth and Timothy became faithful servants of God because they had faithful friends who understood the process of discipleship. Naomi and Paul proved instrumental, not only in introducing these young people to the Lord, but also in helping them grow and understand His ways. Naomi allowed Ruth to accompany her on her journey home, a passive act. But she also invested herself proactively in Ruth's life, by giving her encouragement about gathering the harvest (Ruth 2) and counsel about an important life decision (Ruth 3). Similarly, Paul continued the discipling process, even into Timothy's first pastorate.

The ultimate Discipler is the Holy Spirit, who is called alongside believers in relationship to point to Jesus and make truth known (teaching). The Holy Spirit calls us to accountability and brings encouragement (coaching, cheering, celebrating). The Holy Spirit ushers us into a relationship with the Lord, then He continues to draw us closer to Him every day thereafter. He never quits!

What does it mean to "make a disciple"?

Who has been a significant discipler in your life and how?

Are you actively discipling someone now? If so, how does that relationship work?

Discipleship cannot be confined to an event, a class, a book, a series of lessons, or even a particular period of time. In one sense, it is a lifelong process. Yet, it is also fair to understand the critical phase of discipleship as that initial period of growth following the salvation experience. For Ruth, this, no doubt, took place prior to our meeting her in Scripture. Coming from the completely pagan culture of Moab, Ruth would have needed to learn everything about God.

In today's culture, Christians are assigned a similar mission. What basic facts would you need to teach a completely irreligious person who had just accepted Jesus as her Savior?

How would the process differ if you were discipling a person who had a church background but had just begun a personal relationship with Christ?

Discipleship takes time. Paul's relationship with Timothy demonstrates his willingness to spend time investing in the young pastor's life. In his second letter to Timothy, Paul writes with a great sense of urgency. His sense of how little time he had left personally, his dismay at the challenges of the culture in which Timothy ministered, and his anticipation of the Lord's return strengthened his resolve.

How can you keep a holy sense of urgency?

In light of Christ's soon return, how can you—with the aid of the Spirit—increase the fruit of your discipleship practices?

INVITING GOD TO CHANGE MY VIEW
What change is God asking me to make?

Armed with the gospel in her heart and a tract in her hand, an intrepid third-grader explained salvation to her eager second-grade neighbors. The seven-year-olds were more than willing to listen to the popular older girl, and the time passed quickly on the bus ride to school that day.

Afterwards, in the privacy of their own homes, both girls prayed and invited Christ to be their Lord. Now absent from the picture, the hit-and-run evangelist found other friends on the bus. The girls were left to learn more on their own. One brought a miniature Bible to school, and they eagerly studied it together at recess. It only contained one story, though, and despite their initial enthusiasm and genuine salvation experiences, the girls drifted to more pressing matters, like kickball and cooties.

Sadly, this simple, true tale repeats itself in countless lives every day. A well-meaning Christian shares the gospel with a friend, and because the gospel is true, the Spirit faithful, and personal relationships the most effective form of evangelism, the friend responds favorably. Then the evangelistic friend, celebrating the excitement of reaching another person for Jesus, moves on without completing the good work she has begun.

Jesus commissioned us *to make disciples*. It cannot happen without personal investment. Are you investing yourself intentionally and redemptively in the life of a friend? Ask the Lord to create such opportunities. Do you need to improve a discipling skill, such as listening, teaching, correcting, or encouraging? Would you like to have the heart of a discipler? Do you need to learn how to create space in your schedule for meaningful discipleship? Will you ask the Lord to use you more effectively in discipling others?

Prayer

Lord Jesus, I want to make disciples. I cannot be content with a sporadic evangelistic style. I need to see clearly the people in whom You would like me to invest my life. Help me be the kind of friend of Yours that others want to imitate. Enlarge my heart, Lord, so I am continuously ministering out of a fresh, growing relationship. I am so grateful that You enrich my life with the gift of friendship. Thank You, Lord.

JOURNALING
Take a few minutes to record your personal insights from the lesson.

Her Attitudes in Relationships

CATCHING SIGHT
Introduction

A FAMILIAR STORY about two frogs can teach us a lesson about handling disappointment.

Two frogs fell into a bucket of cream so deep that they could not jump out.

One frog despaired, "What's the use of trying to get out? It must be fate. Good-bye, cruel world!" He gave up and drowned.

The second frog had a different attitude. "I'll try to swim for a while," he said. He swam and kicked persistently until he was able to hop out of the bucket. His kicking had turned the cream into butter.

When we are treated unfairly or someone disappoints us, we are often tempted to run or give up. However, we serve a God who wants us to grow spiritually through such times. When everyone likes us and life just couldn't get any better, being faithful seems almost as easy and natural as breathing. But when the storm comes—when people criticize us, when a relationship disappoints us, when a boss corrects us, when nothing is going right—if we still choose to be faithful then, that's when faithfulness really counts for something.

Remember this story when you are tempted to give up. Many prayers go unanswered because we give up too soon.

GETTING FOCUSED
Begin your study by considering the following:

How do you respond when disappointment comes into your life?

BIBLE READING
2 Timothy 1:15; 2:14–18, 24–26; 4:10, 14–18; 1 John 2:15

New International Version

2 Timothy 1:15 You know that everyone in the province of Asia has deserted me, including Phygelus and Hermogenes.

2:14 Keep reminding them of these things. Warn them before God against quarreling about words; it is of no value, and only ruins those who listen. 15 Do your best to present yourself to God as one approved, a workman who does not need to be ashamed and who correctly handles the word of truth. 16 Avoid godless chatter, because those who indulge in it will become more and more ungodly. 17 Their teaching will spread like gangrene. Among them are Hymenaeus and Philetus, 18 who have wandered away from the truth. They say that the resurrection has already taken place, and they destroy the faith of some.

24 And the Lord's servant must not quarrel; instead, he must be kind to everyone, able to teach, not resentful. 25 Those who oppose him he must gently instruct, in the hope that God will grant them repentance leading them to a knowledge of the truth, 26 and that they will come to

New Living Translation

2 Timothy 1:15 As you know, all the Christians who came here from the province of Asia have deserted me; even Phygelus and Hermogenes are gone.

2:14 Remind everyone of these things, and command them in God's name to stop fighting over words. Such arguments are useless, and they can ruin those who hear them. 15 Work hard so God can approve you. Be a good worker, one who does not need to be ashamed and who correctly explains the word of truth. 16 Avoid godless, foolish discussions that lead to more and more ungodliness. 17 This kind of talk spreads like cancer. Hymenaeus and Philetus are examples of this. 18 They have left the path of truth, preaching the lie that the resurrection of the dead has already occurred; and they have undermined the faith of some.

24 The Lord's servants must not quarrel but must be kind to everyone. They must be able to teach effectively and be patient with difficult people. 25 They should gently teach those who oppose the truth. Perhaps God will change those

New International Version

their senses and escape from the trap of the devil, who has taken them captive to do his will.

4:10 Demas, because he loved this world, has deserted me and has gone to Thessalonica. Crescens has gone to Galatia, and Titus to Dalmatia.

14 Alexander the metalworker did me a great deal of harm. The Lord will repay him for what he has done. 15 You too should be on your guard against him, because he strongly opposed our message.

16 At my first defense, no one came to my support, but everyone deserted me. May it not be held against them. 17 But the Lord stood at my side and gave me strength, so that through me the message might be fully proclaimed and all the Gentiles might hear it. And I was delivered from the lion's mouth. 18 The Lord will rescue me from every evil attack and will bring me safely to his heavenly kingdom. To him be glory for ever and ever. Amen.

1 John 2:15 Do not love the world or anything in the world. If anyone loves the world, the love of the Father is not in him.

New Living Translation

people's hearts, and they will believe the truth. 26 Then they will come to their senses and escape from the Devil's trap. For they have been held captive by him to do whatever he wants.

4:10 Demas has deserted me because he loves the things of this life and has gone to Thessalonica. Crescens has gone to Galatia, and Titus has gone to Dalmatia.

14 Alexander the coppersmith has done me much harm, but the Lord will judge him for what he has done. 15 Be careful of him, for he fought against everything we said.

16 The first time I was brought before the judge, no one was with me. Everyone had abandoned me. I hope it will not be counted against them. 17 But the Lord stood with me and gave me strength, that I might preach the Good News in all its fullness for all the Gentiles to hear. And he saved me from certain death. 18 Yes, and the Lord will deliver me from every evil attack and will bring me safely to his heavenly Kingdom. To God be the glory forever and ever. Amen.

1 John 2:15 Stop loving this evil world and all that it offers you, for when you love the world, you show that you do not have the love of the Father in you.

GAINING BIBLICAL INSIGHT
Maintaining my confidence in God's faithfulness

As we read Paul's writings, we realize he had many friends in different places. Although he seems to have had a very close relationship with most of them, he also had relationships that were disappointing. Most of us will experience some disappointing, or even disillusioning, relationships on our Christian journey. That is when we must maintain our confidence in the faithfulness of God.

Friends Who Forsake Us

We are disappointed when friends fail to support us when we need them. When Paul made his defense in court, none of his friends came to the trial. He mentions two friends, Phygelus and Hermogenes (2 Timothy 1:15), whom he obviously expected to be there. Even these close friends let him down.

In such a circumstance, we might tend to become bitter or to indulge in self-pity because of our friend's actions. Paul dealt with the issue in an entirely different way, following the example of forgiveness shown by Jesus on the cross. "May it not be held against them," he prayed (4:16). Paul shares his testimony that Jesus stood with him when others failed him. When we are aware that God is faithful when others fail, we can have the strength to stand alone.

Friends Who Quarrel about Insignificant Matters

Sometimes, friends get into arguments over insignificant matters, such as the usage of words (2:14). These kinds of arguments have no value, Paul said, and only destroy those who become involved in them. He instructed Timothy to stay out of futile arguments that never come to a resolution.

After instructing Timothy to avoid arguments, he suggested three possible responses that would help him when he faced an explosive situation (verse 24). List them here.

A commitment to kindness in all relationships would help Timothy when conversations became heated. If he knew his friends well and knew what issues produced arguments, Timothy could plan to share information to bring understanding to both sides. Most of all, Paul warned Timothy to guard his spirit against resenting his argumentative friends. Controlling his spirit was more important than proving a point in an argument.

Friends Who Refuse to Confront Issues

Sometimes friends move conversation beyond meaningless arguments into areas that lead to doctrinal error (verse 16). Paul warned Timothy that this kind of conversation can spread rapidly, destroying the faith of those involved in it. He specifically mentions two friends who strayed into error concerning the Resurrection, the doctrine at the heart of the gospel.

How does Paul tell Timothy to deal with friends who stray into doctrinal error?

The first way is to be sure of our own solid knowledge of the Word of God and its teaching (verse 15). Then we are in a position to "gently instruct" others "in the hope that God will grant them repentance leading them to a knowledge of the truth" (verse 25).

Since Timothy lived in Ephesus, he probably knew of the incident that took place in the founding days of his church (Acts 18). Apollos, a dynamic young minister, was preaching the baptism of John. Priscilla and Aquila quietly took him aside and taught him further truth. They gently instructed him privately, rather than publicly confronting him—a good example of dealing with doctrinal error among friends.

Friends Who Love This Present World

Probably one of the most heartrending losses for Paul came when his close friend Demas deserted him. Demas had helped Paul in his ministry for some time. Tragically, Demas not only forsook Paul, but he also turned his back on his Christian faith "because he loved this world" (4:10).

Did keeping up with his imprisoned friend make life difficult for Demas? Did other friends make lucrative offers he could not refuse, causing him to abandon Paul? Did he just want to have some fun, and continually visiting Paul in prison hindered him? We don't know what enticed Demas away from the faith, but these are some reasons present-day Christians fall away.

The apostle John gave helpful counsel to anyone allured by money, pleasure, or an easier life. "Do not love the world or anything in the world. If anyone loves the world, the love of the Father is not in him" (1 John 2:15). John is not talking about having compassion on the people of the world here. Instead, he is talking about loving the world system, which has values contradictory to a Christian worldview. Becoming emotionally attached to the value system of this world is the first step in the wrong direction for Christians.

Friends Who Do Actual Harm

One friend or acquaintance of Paul did actual damage to him. Paul said, "Alexander the metalworker did me a great deal of harm" (2 Timothy 4:14). It may be that Alexander was one of the people Paul mentioned in 1 Timothy 1:19 as having "shipwrecked their faith." Those who lose faith often turn upon the faithful in harmful ways. Paul is probably not talking about physical harm, but damage to his testimony and opportunity for freedom.

When someone hurts us in some way, either personally or by damaging our reputation, our first inclination is to defend ourselves in anger. However, Paul chose to let God deal with the situation. In the same breath, he added, "The Lord will repay him for what he has done" (2 Timothy 4:14).

Paul's faith in God shines through all his disappointing relationships with friends. When others fail us, we can depend on the faithfulness of God.

The relationship between Samson and Delilah is a prime example of one person disappointing another. We can easily see Samson's faults, including repeatedly succumbing to Delilah's charm; however, we can also feel his great disappointment when she betrays him. Let's listen to their story.

REFLECTING HIS IMAGE
Delilah (Judges 16)

Stroking her long, luxurious hair, she reached for the red lip balm on her dressing table and smiled confidently. *I am, after all, extraordinarily beautiful,* she thought. *And I'm a great actress. Why shouldn't I use the power of my sexuality for personal gain?* Delilah was a woman determined to get ahead, and her plan was foolproof.

When Samson began an affair with Delilah, the Philistines seized the opportunity to learn the secret of his amazing physical strength. He had fought and killed hundreds of Philistines, and no force had been able to overcome him. Until now. They offered Delilah a fortune to discover Samson's secret and betray him—an offer she could not refuse.

Close by, Samson awoke from a fretful sleep. As he sat straight up and looked around the room, worry crept into his thoughts, and Delilah's words from the night before washed over him. Nevertheless, a single ray of hope flickered in his heart. He knew he should be wary of her motives, but he had fallen hopelessly in love with Delilah, a choice he feared would be his downfall.

Certainly, if his parents had had their way, he would have married an Israelite. But Samson was a man controlled by his passions. Nothing they said would deter him. Drinking, brawling, and consorting with prostitutes, he knew he'd broken every Nazirite vow—except one. As a Nazirite, his hair had never been cut.

He crawled out of bed and inhaled deeply. Delilah was standing in the doorway. Her beauty took his breath away. "Good morning, Samson," she said. "Sleep well?" He knew by the look in her eye and the bittersweet smile on her face, she wanted something.

She is exceptionally good at pestering, he thought. *But look at her!*

"Samson," she said, "why won't you tell me what makes you so strong? You tricked me with talk of ropes that would not break, and yet they shredded like thread. Then you said braiding your hair would weaken you, and that was a lie." Turning her back to him, her voice quivered and her eyes filled with tears. Time to spin her web until Samson had no place to escape. "Do you enjoy making a fool of me?" she cried. "Because if you truly loved me, you would confide in me!"

Day after day Delilah kept up this line of attack until finally she wore him down. He told her the truth. Whether or not he could trust her remained to be seen, but he knew he could not imagine life without her.

"Delilah," said Samson, "the secret of my strength lies in the fact that, as a Nazirite, my hair has never been cut. I was dedicated to God before I was born. If my hair is ever shaved off, my strength will leave me. Then I'll be like any other man."

Delilah robbed him that very night. At precisely the right moment, waiting until Samson was asleep, she cut his hair and, immediately, his strength was gone.

"Wake up, Samson!" she cried. "The Philistines have come for you." Groggily, Samson looked around and stumbled to his feet, as the army of men hurled taunts, insults, and humiliation at him. They bludgeoned him, blinded him, and dragged him from his house and the woman he loved.

And Delilah stood by and watched it all.

But so did God. Without her knowledge or consent, God used her actions for good. He knew Samson's scars and disappointment ran deep from this love-hate relationship. Eventually, God's anger brought the Philistines' temple down on their own heads—through Samson.

EMBRACING THE PENTECOSTAL PERSPECTIVE
What is the Holy Spirit teaching me?

What a fool! is exactly what Samson must have been thinking of himself, and he was right. Yes, he should have stayed away from Delilah. He should have married an Israelite woman. He should have listened to his family. Hindsight can be cruel, but the disappointments of the past must not control the future!

Paul never stopped building new friendships, even when others let him down. He did not stop mentoring ministers like Timothy and

Titus, even when other friends abandoned him. Instead, Paul focused on the future, refusing to indulge in the bitter clarity of hindsight. He did not permit the mistakes of one person to speak for the character of all.

How is the Spirit's assigned task of "pointing to Jesus" helpful when friends let us down?

What is the best way to get over the pain of a friend's hurtful actions?

How can we continue to believe the best of others when we have experienced some of the worst?

Paul never laid the blame for others' failings at God's feet. When people hurt, they often bypass the guilty party and go directly to God, crediting Him with people's sins. For example, how often did you hear God blamed for the events of September 11, rather than the terrorists who planned and performed the deed? God deserves the credit for a great many things—but never sin. God is good. God is faithful. He never abandons us.

Do you need to let God "off the hook" for something you have falsely accused Him of?

How has the Lord shown His faithfulness in your life recently?

What would you say to a friend who is blaming God for her own or another's failures? What do you say when there is no one to blame?

Trust grows better friendships than cynicism does. You cannot protect yourself from disappointment by anticipating failure. Relationships always involve risk. We risk investing ourselves in the lives of others with no guarantee of favorable, or even faithful, response. Happily, the benefits of friendship far outweigh the risks!

What happens to friendship when trust is withheld?

Do you rely on the Spirit's leading in all of your relationships? How so?

INVITING GOD TO CHANGE MY VIEW
What change is God asking me to make?

Rubbing his tired eyes, Peter must have done a double take when he saw the Lord on the distant shore (John 21). After one of the most difficult times in his life, Peter was probably in no mood for another disappointment. Still reeling from his betrayal of the Lord, the horror of the Crucifixion, and sorting out the reality of the Resurrection, the hoped-for simplicity of the fishing excursion had proved dismally nontherapeutic. Now, if he was not mistaken, the Lord offered friendship, and more importantly, forgiveness.

Second chances are rare, especially when the relational rift cuts as deeply as Peter's denials. But Jesus exemplifies the power of God's faithfulness. He reached out to Peter in a personal and pointed way. Jesus went to him, not once, but repeatedly. He did not rehearse the past, but pointed to the future. He offered trust. Peter grew in his relationship with the Lord, fulfilled his call to ministry, and impacted the world.

Guarding our hearts from bitterness and keeping faith in the Lord are essential for spiritual health, but they are not the only issues involved when a friend disappoints. Like Jesus, we may have an opportunity for restoration. It is not always possible, as Paul's experiences demonstrate, but we should always consider the possibility. So much is at stake! Reaching out to a friend who has broken faith may bridge the path to a Spirit-empowered future of untold value.

Do you hold God responsible for the unfaithfulness of someone? Do you need a fresh filling of the Holy Spirit to extend forgiveness to another? Have you disappointed God or others and not found the courage to make it right? Will you allow the Lord to bring restoration to your faith and relationships?

Prayer

Heavenly Father, I believe You will never leave or forsake me. You are faithful. When others are not, I pray for the grace to forgive. May Your Spirit have easy access to my heart to lead me to You for comfort, assurance, and direction. Help me never to allow disappointments with others to cloud my vision of You. Help me be the kind of friend Jesus was to Peter, to have the unshakable faith of Paul, and to never use a friend as Delilah did Samson. I ask it in Jesus' name. Amen.

JOURNALING

Take a few minutes to record your personal insights from the lesson.

Her Relationship to the World System

CATCHING SIGHT

Introduction

MIRACULOUS! REVOLUTIONARY! GREATEST EVER! We are inundated by extravagant claims as we flip through television channels or magazine pages. Messages leap out at us, assuring us the advertised products are new and improved—capable of changing our lives. For only a few dollars, we can have cleaner clothes, whiter teeth, more glamorous hair, and tastier food. Cars, perfume, diet drinks, and mouthwash are guaranteed to bring happiness, friends, and the good life. And just before an election, no advertisement's claims can match the politicians' promises. But talk is cheap, and too often we realize the boasts were hollow and far from the truth.

To keep ourselves from being polluted, we must commit ourselves to Christ's ethical and moral system instead of the world's, which is based on money, power, and pleasure. True faith means nothing if we are contaminated by such values.

No one imagined Charles Dutton could achieve anything, because he spent many years imprisoned for manslaughter. But when some-one asked this now-successful Broadway star of *The Piano Lesson* how he managed to make such a remarkable transition, he replied, "Unlike the other prisoners, I never decorated my cell."[1]

Dutton had resolved never to regard his prison cell as home. Christians will accomplish much in this world when they don't accus-tom themselves to it, but instead are "longing for a better country" (Hebrews 11:16), a heavenly one.

---

[1] Craig Brian Larson, ed., *Illustrations for Preaching and Teaching: From Leadership Journal* (Grand Rapids: Baker Books, 1993), 280.

GETTING FOCUSED

Begin your study by considering the following:

What worldly interest seems to have a stronger hold on you than you know is healthy for a Christian?

BIBLE READING

2 Timothy 3:1–16

New International Version

1 But mark this: There will be terrible times in the last days. 2 People will be lovers of themselves, lovers of money, boastful, proud, abusive, disobedient to their parents, ungrateful, unholy, 3 without love, unforgiving, slanderous, without self-control, brutal, not lovers of the good, 4 treacherous, rash, conceited, lovers of pleasure rather than lovers of God—5 having a form of godliness but denying its power. Have nothing to do with them.

6 They are the kind who worm their way into homes and gain control over weak-willed women, who are loaded down with sins and are swayed by all kinds of evil desires, 7 always learning but never able to acknowledge the truth. 8 Just as Jannes and Jambres opposed Moses, so also these men oppose the truth—men of depraved minds, who, as far as the faith is concerned, are rejected. 9 But they will not get very far because, as in the case of those men, their folly will be clear to everyone.

New Living Translation

1 You should also know this, Timothy, that in the last days there will be very difficult times. 2 For people will love only themselves and their money. They will be boastful and proud, scoffing at God, disobedient to their parents, and ungrateful. They will consider nothing sacred. 3 They will be unloving and unforgiving; they will slander others and have no self-control; they will be cruel and have no interest in what is good. 4 They will betray their friends, be reckless, be puffed up with pride, and love pleasure rather than God. 5 They will act as if they are religious, but they will reject the power that could make them godly. You must stay away from people like that.

6 They are the kind who work their way into people's homes and win the confidence of vulnerable women who are burdened with the guilt of sin and controlled by many desires. 7 Such women are forever following new teachings, but they never understand the truth. 8 And these teachers fight the truth just as

New International Version

10 You, however, know all about my teaching, my way of life, my purpose, faith, patience, love, endurance, 11 persecutions, sufferings—what kinds of things happened to me in Antioch, Iconium and Lystra, the persecutions I endured. Yet the Lord rescued me from all of them. 12 In fact, everyone who wants to live a godly life in Christ Jesus will be persecuted, 13 while evil men and impostors will go from bad to worse, deceiving and being deceived. 14 But as for you, continue in what you have learned and have become convinced of, because you know those from whom you learned it, 15 and how from infancy you have known the holy Scriptures, which are able to make you wise for salvation through faith in Christ Jesus. 16 All Scripture is God-breathed and is useful for teaching, rebuking, correcting and training in righteousness.

New Living Translation

Jannes and Jambres fought against Moses. Their minds are depraved, and their faith is counterfeit. 9 But they won't get away with this for long. Someday everyone will recognize what fools they are, just as happened with Jannes and Jambres.

10 But you know what I teach, Timothy, and how I live, and what my purpose in life is. You know my faith and how long I have suffered. You know my love and my patient endurance. 11 You know how much persecution and suffering I have endured. You know all about how I was persecuted in Antioch, Iconium, and Lystra—but the Lord delivered me from all of it. 12 Yes, and everyone who wants to live a godly life in Christ Jesus will suffer persecution. 13 But evil people and impostors will flourish. They will go on deceiving others, and they themselves will be deceived.

14 But you must remain faithful to the things you have been taught. You know they are true, for you know you can trust those who taught you. 15 You have been taught the holy Scriptures from childhood, and they have given you the wisdom to receive the salvation that comes by trusting in Christ Jesus. 16 All Scripture is inspired by God and is useful to teach us what is true and to make us realize what is wrong in our lives. It straightens us out and teaches us to do what is right.

GAINING BIBLICAL INSIGHT
Challenging my culture with godly living

A cursory reading of 2 Timothy 3 may remind us of accounts printed in our daily newspaper. Paul warned the young Timothy of "terrible times in the last days" (verse 1). Though the description of these days reminds us of our own times, Paul was referring to the entire Messianic period, beginning with Christ's birth. We know these problems were prevalent already in the days of the Early Church, because Paul warned Timothy not to be involved with these kinds of people (verse 5).

Problems Faced in the Present World System

The centuries have brought many changes in technology which have affected our lifestyles. However, human nature has not changed a great deal—people were much the same in Paul's day as they are today.

In listing the problems of the world system, Paul dealt first with the area of people's affections.

Read 2 Timothy 3:1–9. List three things Paul said people in the last days will love and two they will not love.

Notice how people's affections influence their lifestyles. Many of the negative actions Paul listed spring from self-centeredness, resulting in heartless disregard for the treatment of others.

Other misdirected affections, such as the love of money and the love of pleasure, are only extensions of self-love. Excessive materialism is a result of self-gratification, as is the disproportionate quest for pleasure. The root problem of the people mentioned in this passage was the combination of their inward focus and their lack of concern for others or God. Self ruled on the throne of their hearts.

In the passage, Paul listed two areas where love was absent among these people, further indicating their self-centeredness. They did not love basic moral goodness, nor did they love God. They tried to mask this absence with a form of godliness that lacked the presence or power of God.

In addition to self-centered affections, Paul referred to another problem area—their handling of truth.

What is their relationship to truth, according to verses 7 and 8?

The self-centered living Paul describes in this passage is the result of rejected truth. These people did not simply ignore truth; they also opposed it, because of their depraved minds. As you read through this section, pick up a copy of your daily newspaper. Compare what you read about human nature in Timothy's day to what is happening in our world. Like Timothy, we are surrounded by an ungodly world system and we need to know how to relate to it.

Paul's Example and Teaching for Coping with the System

Because of Paul's love and concern for Timothy, he warned Timothy about the kinds of people he would meet and gave him some advice for coping with the system.

First, Paul reminded Timothy of the differences between his teaching and the depraved thinking of the people Timothy could encounter. Timothy had traveled with Paul and had heard him preach on many occasions. Adding Paul's teaching to his own background in Old Testament Scriptures, Timothy had a solid knowledge of God's Word to support his Christian faith. Paul wanted him to keep this teaching in the forefront of his mind. Having a mind shaped by the Word of God is a great antidote to the corrupt thinking of an ungodly world system.

Paul then rehearsed his own lifestyle for Timothy, pointing out how it backed up his teaching. He focused on the positive manifestations of his faith—purposeful living, integrity, patience, love, and endurance. These are the same characteristics Paul wanted Timothy to possess, in contrast to the self-centered lifestyles around him. In referring to his positive characteristics, Paul was not boasting, but recognizing the goodness of God in his life.

Paul knew living for Christ in an ungodly environment would be difficult for Timothy, as it is for Christians today. So he reminded Timothy of some of the events that had happened in his travels. Paul had been stoned in Lystra, Timothy's hometown. Timothy knew very well what Paul suffered there. Paul did not want Timothy to be surprised if suffering also came to him (verse 12). He reminded Timothy of God's faithfulness to rescue His children in suffering (verse 11).

Principles to Follow for Living within the System

Paul shared principles with Timothy to help him live within a contrary world system. These same principles will strengthen people today who struggle to live godly lives in an ungodly environment.

Paul pointed to the Word of God as the foundation for his Christian life. He wanted Timothy to make the Word the solid foundation of his life also. Paul affirmed that the Scriptures are inspired by God. This concept is vital to our understanding and appreciation of Scripture as the infallible Word of God.

What four ways does Paul say the Scriptures are useful?

The Scripture is our source of truth. As such, it is the guide that reveals our errors and shows us the correct way to live. It equips us for usefulness in the kingdom of God. Paul was teaching Timothy the possibilities of influencing the culture by godly living, rather than letting the culture shape us.

The New Testament Church witnessed how God dealt with two of its members who became too much a part of the world around them. Let's hear from friends of Sapphira how her deception impacted them.

REFLECTING HIS IMAGE
Sapphira (Acts 5:1–11)

The knock on my front door could not have come at a more inconvenient time. I was busy with my chores. Another knock—louder, harder. I wiped the dripping water from my hands on my apron and answered the door. My sister stood in the doorway, shaking and weeping uncontrollably.

"I'm sorry to bother you so close to mealtime, but I don't know where else to go. Can we talk for a moment, please?" I invited her in, and as she sat down at the table, the quiver in her voice let me know something awful had happened. I offered a cup of cold water to help her regain her composure.

"Tell me how I can help you," I finally said.

"She's dead," she cried. "Sapphira is dead! Ananias too!"

Except for my sister's sobbing, all I heard was the stillness of my own inner voice. My thoughts raced ahead before she could even continue her story. Sapphira, our friend—dead? Inconceivable!

She and her husband were strong believers, active members of the vibrant and exciting Jerusalem church where prayer, worship, and fellowship were commonplace. They were the ideal couple. They had the "ideal" marriage. *At least, that's the way it seemed*, I thought. *What could possibly have happened?*

My sister broke down again. Numb to my own emotion, I sat beside her, held her, and comforted her. Finally, after several minutes, she continued her story.

"Sapphira and Ananias devised a horrible plan to deceive the Church. Like others in our community, they sold property and brought the money to the apostle Peter. But, apparently, the two of them talked it over and decided to keep part of the proceeds, while pretending to give it all. Peter wanted to know the price of the property, and Ananias lied. He was immediately struck dead and carried out. Later, Sapphira came in and Peter asked her the same question. And she lied, too! She dropped dead. My dear friend lied. How could she do such a thing? Now she's dead . . . dead."

The next hour was a blur as I tried my best to console someone who was inconsolable. I found myself trying to speak, but realized I had no idea what to say to my young sister, who had been so deceived and disappointed by her trusted friend. I knew by the shocked, blank stare on her face that, finally, the hollow reality of what had happened had sunk in. Sapphira was gone. She was never coming back. She would be missed.

Some circumstances in life cause wounds so grievous, they cannot be soothed with mere words.

Sapphira had so many blessings: a good marriage, a loving church with warm and caring relationships, financial security. Yet, she wanted more. I guess her concern for appearances and impressing others was her final undoing. Her "holy act" became a mockery and offended the Holy Spirit.

Time passed and healing did come to my sister, slowly. At first she felt God's sentence passed on Ananias and Sapphira was too severe. But with time, she came to understand that pretense is never acceptable to the Holy Spirit.

"You know," she said to me, not too long ago, "I'm tempted at times, just like Sapphira, to make myself look like someone I'm not—more forgiving, more generous, more loving than I really am. Losing my friend is teaching me that, while I might fool others, I can't fool God."

How wise for someone so young, I thought. *True and wise indeed.*

EMBRACING THE PENTECOSTAL PERSPECTIVE
What is the Holy Spirit teaching me?

If she had been duped, we might sympathize. But the biblical account tells us Sapphira had full knowledge (Acts 5:2). That means she had a choice: tell the truth or lie; serve the Kingdom or seek personal gain; love God first or love money more. It sounds so black and white, but Sapphira probably blurred those lines with several small choices before she launched into life-or-death territory.

We have the same choices today. Jesus clearly taught that we should love God with our whole heart, mind, soul, and strength. He warned that we could not love both God and money, possessions could not be more valuable than promise and purpose, and our way could not be more important than God's will. What will you choose to be—friend of God or friend of the world? It is a "no-brainer" when the decision is worded that way. If only it were always that simple.

What kinds of affection for this world tend to get in the way of that choice?

How can you more quickly recognize the pull of the world?

How does the Spirit give us the strength to extricate ourselves from that pull?

Paul spent a significant portion of his letter encouraging Timothy to live a godly life. He pointed out specific behaviors to imitate and avoid, referred him to the Word of God for ongoing direction, and showed the benefits of a godly life. While we ought to be doing the same for others, we also need the reminder ourselves.

Do you refer to God's Word to understand contemporary problems? Give an example.

Share an experience in which choosing godliness over world-liness brought blessing to your life.

Has the Spirit helped you endure persecution for your faith? If so, how?

Christians, at times, have been guilty of a "hold-the-fort" mental-ity in relationship to the world. They have viewed the Church as a pitiful huddle, cowering in fear of the enemy, struggling to preserve the light of a single candle. This horrific distortion of biblical truth cripples the Church, keeping it from fulfilling God's intentions. The Church Jesus described in the New Testament kicks down the gates of hell, marches into the enemy's territory, and extends the love of God with miraculous, redemptive results. A biblical worldview, informed by a vibrant life in the Lord, enables you to operate from Jesus' teach-ing of strength, rather than fear, in relationship to the world.

What is your current posture toward the world? Do you huddle away from it or do you march into it with godly intent?

How can Spirit-filled believers impact the world for Christ? Are you Spirit-filled? Are you impacting your world? How?

What can we say to believers who condemn the world with no thought whatsoever for its salvation?

INVITING GOD TO CHANGE MY VIEW
What change is God asking me to make?

It worked last week; why not now? she wondered. The porch light remained dark, despite multiple repair efforts. She had tested and replaced the bulb, removed debris, and even detached the fixture to check the wiring. Everything looked good, but somehow the power failed to connect. *What good is a porch light that doesn't illuminate the porch?*

Good question. While some may decorate with faux fixtures, most of us want the real deal. If a light is connected to a power source, it ought to work! Likewise, if we are connected in divine relationship to our Savior, we cannot be content with anything that simply *appears* godly but has no real power. Why settle for a relationship with our Savior that is devoid of conversation or lacking the fullness of the Spirit as demonstrated by the gifts, fruit, and power of the Spirit?

If we are careless about our relationship to the world, we will grow careless in our relationship with the Lord. At that juncture, an opportunity exists for deceiving ourselves and others about the reality found in Christ. We cannot afford that deception. Prayers that do not effect change, people with stagnant spiritual lives, and Spirit-filled believers who are not impacting their world are all empty forms and do not reflect God's plan for His people.

Are you holding too tightly to some element of the world? Do you need to find freedom from bondage? Are you propping up an empty form of godliness in your life? Will you ask the Lord for grace and a fresh infilling of His Spirit to live in His power? Do you need boldness to impact your world? Do you need a Christian worldview?

Prayer

Lord Jesus, thank You for showing me how to live a godly life in this world. I know I do not have to live in fear or isolation. Show me how to best shine Your light in this darkened place. I do not want to hide or extinguish Your light. Through Your Spirit, lead me to those who need You. Give me discernment to see the difference between godly and ungodly acts. As I draw closer to You, Lord, let me increase in useful-ness to You. I love You, Jesus. Amen.

JOURNALING

Take a few minutes to record your personal insights from the lesson.

Her Relationship to Herself

CATCHING SIGHT

Introduction

H EALTHY SELF-ESTEEM IS important for everyone. Some of us think too little of ourselves. On the other hand, some of us overestimate our abilities. The key to an honest and accurate evaluation is knowing the basis of our self-worth—our identity in Christ.

An Olympic diver was asked how he coped with the stress of international diving competitions. He described how he climbs to the board, takes a deep breath, and thinks, *Even if I blow this dive, my mother will still love me.* Then he strives for excellence!

Apart from Christ, we aren't capable of accomplishing very much by eternal standards, but in Him we are valuable and capable of worthy service. Evaluating yourself by the worldly standards of success and achievement can cause you to think too much about your worth in the eyes of others. You could miss your true value in God's eyes.

Some women take the love and grace of God for granted. At the beginning of each day, take a deep breath and say, "Even if I blow it today, God will still love me." Then, assured of grace, go into the day striving for excellence!

GETTING FOCUSED

Begin your study by considering the following:

What is it about yourself that makes you feel unworthy? In light of your position in Christ, should that evaluation change?

BIBLE READING
2 Timothy 4:6–22

New International Version

6 For I am already being poured out like a drink offering, and the time has come for my departure. 7 I have fought the good fight, I have finished the race, I have kept the faith. 8 Now there is in store for me the crown of righteousness, which the Lord, the righteous Judge, will award to me on that day—and not only to me, but also to all who have longed for his appearing.

9 Do your best to come to me quickly, 10 for Demas, because he loved this world, has deserted me and has gone to Thessalonica. Crescens has gone to Galatia, and Titus to Dalmatia. 11 Only Luke is with me. Get Mark and bring him with you, because he is helpful to me in my ministry. 12 I sent Tychicus to Ephesus. 13 When you come, bring the cloak that I left with Carpus at Troas, and my scrolls, especially the parchments.

14 Alexander the metalworker did me a great deal of harm. The Lord will repay him for what he has done. 15 You too should be on your guard against him, because he strongly opposed our message.

16 At my first defense, no one came to my support, but everyone deserted me. May it not be held against them. 17 But the Lord stood at my side and gave me strength, so

New Living Translation

6 As for me, my life has already been poured out as an offering to God. The time of my death is near. 7 I have fought a good fight, I have finished the race, and I have remained faithful. 8 And now the prize awaits me—the crown of righteousness that the Lord, the righteous Judge, will give me on that great day of his return. And the prize is not just for me but for all who eagerly look forward to his glorious return.

9 Please come as soon as you can. 10 Demas has deserted me because he loves the things of this life and has gone to Thessalonica. Crescens has gone to Galatia, and Titus has gone to Dalmatia. 11 Only Luke is with me. Bring Mark with you when you come, for he will be helpful to me. 12 I sent Tychicus to Ephesus. 13 When you come, be sure to bring the coat I left with Carpus at Troas. Also bring my books, and especially my papers.

14 Alexander the coppersmith has done me much harm, but the Lord will judge him for what he has done. 15 Be careful of him, for he fought against everything we said.

16 The first time I was brought before the judge, no one was with me. Everyone had abandoned me. I hope it will not be counted against them. 17 But the Lord stood with me

New International Version

that through me the message might be fully proclaimed and all the Gentiles might hear it. And I was delivered from the lion's mouth. 18 The Lord will rescue me from every evil attack and will bring me safely to his heavenly kingdom. To him be glory for ever and ever. Amen.

19 Greet Priscilla and Aquila and the household of Onesiphorus. 20 Erastus stayed in Corinth, and I left Trophimus sick in Miletus. 21 Do your best to get here before winter. Eubulus greets you, and so do Pudens, Linus, Claudia and all the brothers.

22 The Lord be with your spirit. Grace be with you.

New Living Translation

and gave me strength, that I might preach the Good News in all its fullness for all the Gentiles to hear. And he saved me from certain death. 18 Yes, and the Lord will deliver me from every evil attack and will bring me safely to his heavenly Kingdom. To God be the glory forever and ever. Amen.

19 Give my greetings to Priscilla and Aquila and those living at the household of Onesiphorus. 20 Erastus stayed at Corinth, and I left Trophimus sick at Miletus.

21 Hurry so you can get here before winter. Eubulus sends you greetings, and so do Pudens, Linus, Claudia, and all the brothers and sisters.

22 May the Lord be with your spirit. Grace be with you all.

GAINING BIBLICAL INSIGHT
Understanding myself in light of God's truth

Our study of relationships would be incomplete if we didn't consider our relationship with ourselves. The capacity to be self-aware is unique to human beings. None of God's other creatures can examine themselves as we can. One of our most difficult tasks in building relationships is maintaining the right attitude toward ourselves.

Paul's writings reveal his awareness of who he was in Christ, which affected his attitude toward his circumstances and his future. From Paul, we can learn principles to help us develop a healthy relationship with ourselves.

Paul's View of Himself

In the opening statement of this letter to Timothy, Paul identifies himself as an apostle (1:1). He used this description of himself most frequently, though at times he used the word *servant* and even *prisoner.* From the use of these words, we understand how he viewed himself. Paul accepted his apostleship, his servanthood, and his situation as a prisoner, because he related every descriptive phrase to his relationship with Christ.

Identifying ourselves can be a difficult exercise. We sometimes describe ourselves in occupational terms, such as *teacher, nurse,* or *stay-at-home mom.* At other times, we describe ourselves in relational terms. We are somebody's *daughter, wife, mother, employee, neighbor,* or *friend.* Accepting our life's circumstance with ease may be related to our ability to add the phrase "of Christ" to the way we define ourselves.

Imagine you are writing a letter to a friend, using Paul's style. Start with your name and add a descriptive term. Can you truthfully add the phrase, "of Christ by the will of God," to this description? Try this exercise with your different roles and relationships. Viewing our position in life as prescribed by Christ is a foundation for healthy self-relationship.

Paul's View of the Past

When Paul wrote this letter to Timothy, Paul knew he was approaching the end of his life—a view which is revealed in his image of the drink offering (4:6). This offering accompanied other offerings in the Old Testament sacrificial system (Numbers 15:5). He viewed his life as a sacrificial offering to God, following Christ's example of sacrifice.

Sacrificial living is a prevailing theme in Paul's writings to the churches. One of the most familiar examples is Romans 12:1, in which he implores believers to present their bodies as living sacrifices.

How did Paul's view of life affect the way he lived?

How can this view of life change the way you live?

Viewing his life as an offering enabled Paul to accept the impending end of his life (2 Timothy 4:6,7). He compared his life to that of a soldier and an athlete who victoriously completed their missions. He achieved personal victory by keeping the faith he had received by revelation on the road to Damascus. Paul could accept his certain death, because he knew he had lived his life faithfully.

How we view life affects our view of death. When we have a healthy relationship with ourselves, we understand our own vulnerability, the fragility of our life, and the certainty of our death. Keeping this view in mind helps us value each moment and live with purpose, so in our later years we can be satisfied with how we have lived.

Paul's View of the Future

Paul also talked about the hope of a future life with the Lord. He continued using the image of the runner, writing about the wreath given to the winner of the race. Paul knew God would be the One giving out rewards at the end of life, not only for him, but for everyone who faithfully served the Lord. This hope sustained him in the difficult times.

How does living with hope affect our relationship with ourselves?

Victor Frankl, a survivor of German concentration camps, observed that when people gave up hope, they gave up the will to live. Even when present circumstances are unbearable, the hope of a brighter future can sustain us. When we see ourselves in Christ with a hope for

the future, we can endure whatever the present brings. We can maintain our sense of self-worth because we have hope of a future reward.

Paul's Present Need

A positive view of the past and a hopeful view of the future do not
take away our awareness of present needs. Paul had very real needs as
a prisoner, but his personal needs could be met only by friends. Some
friends had forsaken him, and he needed the support of Timothy. "Do
your best to come to me quickly," he wrote to Timothy (4:9).

All of us are social creatures. While we need some time alone, we
also need the support and strength of our friends. Our friends are
like mirrors in which we see reflections of ourselves. People who are
highly self-aware can also reach out to build relationships with others.

Paul needed Timothy to minister to both his physical and intel-
lectual needs. "Bring the cloak," he asked, "and my scrolls, especially
the parchments" (4:13). He was not embarrassed to share his personal
needs with his friend.

Sometimes we are hesitant to share needs with friends, thinking we should be independent enough to take care of ourselves. We
like to be on the giving end of friendship, but sometimes we need to
humble ourselves and receive from others. A person with a healthy
self-relationship understands the give-and-take of friendship and can
comfortably express needs to friends.

Paul's Confidence in Christ

Though Paul had a healthy self-relationship, he was not totally self-
reliant. He realized his strength came from the Lord. When it seemed
everyone abandoned him, the Lord was faithful.

Read verses 17 and 18, noting Paul's confidence that the Lord had
rescued him in the past and would do so again in the future. The Lord
was the One who gave his life purpose and the promise of a future in
heaven. This confidence in Christ culminated in joyous praise. Paul's
experience can be ours as we view ourselves positively because of our
relationship to Christ.

This same faith is seen in the life of the woman with the oil. Let's
hear her story.

REFLECTING HIS IMAGE
The Woman with the Oil (2 Kings 4:1–7)

People don't usually die without any warning at all, but I guess my husband didn't know that. One morning, without apparent cause, he dropped dead. Suddenly, I was a widow with children to raise and debts to pay.

Please understand. My husband was a good man who loved God. But the fact was, we were poor, and in order to pay our debts, our creditor was coming to take my two sons as his slaves. Desperate circumstances call for desperate measures, so I asked my husband's teacher, the prophet Elisha, to help me.

That was the day I learned a whole new way of looking at my faith.

Instead of paying off my debt or asking my creditor to cancel it, Elisha asked me two questions: "How can I help you?" and "What do you have in your house?" That was all. The first answer seemed rather obvious, but the second question brought up a more serious issue.

I looked around my house, appraised the situation, and realized the only real asset I had was a jar of olive oil. Can you imagine? A jar of oil!

"This is all I can find," I told Elisha. I still remember how flushed my face was and how my heart raced as I held out the small jar in my hand.

Elisha seemed unaffected by the amount of my meager offering.

"Send your two sons to borrow as many empty containers as they can carry," he said. "Then, fill the containers with your oil."

I know. Sounds strange—to say the least—but I was determined to follow Elisha's advice.

As my children brought jars into the house from around the neighborhood, I began to fill them with oil from my own container. Picture this scene in your mind. With my family close by and looking on, I stood at my table and poured, and poured, and poured. I filled and filled the jars—until none was left empty. Only then did the oil stop flowing. It was incredible!

Then Elisha told me to sell the oil, pay my creditor, and live on the leftover money. A masterful plan orchestrated by God. And to think I was a part of the solution to my own bleak situation, simply because I followed Elisha's advice.

When everything around me seemed dark and hopeless, I asked for help and watched God miraculously save my family from poverty and me from utter despair.

How like God to give me more than I could possibly ask or think!

EMBRACING THE PENTECOSTAL PERSPECTIVE
What is the Holy Spirit teaching me?

Take a closer look at how we are introduced to this widow. She is a wife, a mother, a servant, a woman in crisis. Some would scorn the way her identification of self is described only in relationship to another person or situation, but if you read this woman's testimony and fail to recognize *her* incredible faith and tenacity, you have not understood her at all.

Women often identify themselves in relationship to others: Joe's wife, Jane's mother, a schoolteacher, a cancer survivor. And while all of these are significant roles, they do not get to the heart of who she really is. *Who are you in Christ Jesus?* Answer that question and you will understand yourself, your relationships, and your purpose in life.

What does it mean to be "in Christ Jesus"? (How do we come into this relationship? What privileges do we have? What are our responsibilities?)

Do you ever adopt an indecisive posture toward your identity as a Christian and any other role in your life—failing to allow the Lord to influence your roles in relationships or work? If so, how can you move toward an undivided heart?

Understanding who you are in Christ—a servant, gifted and called to high purpose—compels you to be a person of great faith. When the widow was instructed to borrow jars from her neighbors, she was told specifically, "Don't ask for just a few" (2 Kings 4:3). In other words, "Go big, think big, dream big!" In ourselves, we do not have this capacity, but filled with the Holy Spirit, we can live with the boldness and obedience that lead to God-sized possibilities.

Do you consider yourself a person of great faith? Why or why not?

Put yourself in the widow's story. What hurdle would be hardest for you to leap: the discouragement of the situation, the difficulty of asking for help, the ability to see anything good or useful at your disposal, the humility to borrow from others, or the faith to keep on pouring?

Are you asking the Spirit to lead you to new growth in your faith?

Healthy self-understanding cannot be shaped by others' perspectives, but it is not entirely independent of them, either. For example, if your coworkers think your faith is ridiculous, you should not stop believing. Nor should you isolate yourself from them. Paul did not consider himself a failure because Demas walked away or Alexander attacked him. He understood himself in light of God's perspective, not others' opinions. Yet, even when those opinions were negative, he continued to reach out. Paul and the widow teach us no person is an island.

Paul's closing comments to Timothy included poignant requests for help. When you are distressed, do you ask for help? Why or why not?

Paul left his enemies in the Lord's hands. Why is this so difficult?

Paul pressed close to the Lord. How does the Spirit help you do the same?

INVITING GOD TO CHANGE MY VIEW
What change is God asking me to make?

Many professions have borrowed a concept from the sports world, known as "leaving it all on the field." In numerous movie and television program plots, the characters face a pivotal moment, and their response ultimately affects the outcome of the drama. In this turning point, the players determine to go for an against-all-odds victory, giving it everything they've got.

Long before this timeless principle found its way into pop culture, it was demonstrated by some people with serious faith. Jesus left it all on the field when He came to this earth. He lived a sinless life, went to the cross in our place, and declared, "It is finished." Just prior to his own finish line, Paul testified of having left it all on the field by comparing his life to a drink offering poured out (2 Timothy 4:6).

What about you? Do you have a desire to leave it all on the field? If so, you need to know a few prerequisites. First, you have to see yourself as a player—someone who can make a difference. Next, you have to see the possibility of victory. Act with faith, even when your sight makes that difficult. Last, you must suspend the instinct to hold back. Jesus gave everything. Paul gave everything. Will you?

Do you need a better understanding of who you are in Christ? Do you need to be delivered from the habit of self-criticism? Are you isolating yourself from others or God? Do you need to understand more about your place in God's plan? Will you ask the Lord to pour you out in fulfillment of His call on your life?

Prayer

Father, show me what You see in me. Let me glimpse the hope You have for my potential in Christ Jesus. Protect me from vanity and self-centered thoughts and actions. May Your Spirit quickly point out anything within me that stinks of self-pride. Use me, Father. Use all I am. Help me not to hold back anything from You. I will trust You for energy, power, faith, and courage to pursue anything You lead me to. I want to please You alone. Blessed be Your Name!

JOURNALING

Take a few minutes to record your personal insights from the lesson.

HOW TO LEAD A BIBLE STUDY GROUP

Welcome to the *Unlimited! . . . Bible Studies for Today's Pentecostal Woman* series! You will find these studies to be a great resource for biblical guidance in living a Christian life in today's unsteady world and for learning more about the Holy Spirit's work in your life.

Leading a group in studying these lessons will be challenging and rewarding as together you discover how to apply God's Word to your life. You may have some questions about leading a Bible study. This section gives direction for answering the "why, who, what, where, when, and how" questions. Let's look at them individually.

"WHY" QUESTIONS
Why have a Bible study?

The first question you may ask is "Why do we want to have a Bible study?" This series is based on biblical, textual information, meant to be an expository study of what God's Word says on the topics presented in each lesson. Bill Bright, in his book *Discover the Book God Wrote*, says, "The Bible is so interconnected with God that we cannot separate it from His being. In fact, when we read the Bible with the right attitude, God, in the person of the Holy Spirit, joins with our spirit to help us understand it and apply it. The Book comes alive! The words in the Bible have life-changing power."[1]

Bible study group dynamics differ from other small group dynamics. Bible study is not necessarily easy, nor should those studying the Bible try to make it easy. Your main goal for beginning a Bible study

---

[1] Bill Bright, *Discover the Book God Wrote* (Wheaton, Ill.: Tyndale House , 2003), 5.

should not be for a group to have fellowship, although fellowship will occur. If your main purpose is something other than a direct study of God's Word to gain biblical understanding for each member's life today, you may want to consider a different curriculum and format. The main goal of Bible study is to understand the Bible in a more profound way, so it will penetrate deeply into the hearts of those attending.

Bible study differs from traditional small groups in that fellowship can happen before and after the study, but not necessarily during. The Bible study sessions may become intense at times while group members grapple with the life issues presented in these lessons. Lives will be changed as a result of understanding God's Word.

If you combine Bible study with the small group dynamics of worship, prayer, and fellowship, then take that into consideration when planning the length of time for your sessions. Be sure the Bible study time is not crowded out by other activities.

"WHO" QUESTIONS

Who are the study members?

Who are you going to invite to this study? Many possibilities exist for establishing a Bible study group: neighbors (presenting evangelism possibilities), a new converts' study, a working women's study, or an intergenerational study. Answering this question helps answer some of the other questions.

Determine if you are going to limit the size of the group and whether you are going to allow newcomers to this study once it has started. A recommended size would be no less than four and no more than eleven members. A study group of twelve or more should be divided into smaller groups to facilitate discussion.

Who is the leadership?

Another "who" question is answered by determining who makes up the leadership of this study group. Will more than one person be a facilitator (teacher)? Will you need others in leadership? For example, do you want a group secretary to keep information such as names, addresses, and e-mail addresses of group members in order to get information to each group member? Do you want a refreshment coordinator or special events coordinator if refreshments or fellowship events are to be a part of your time together? Who will these leaders be? These questions should be determined with the help of your church leadership. The women chosen for these positions need to be mature Christians.

"WHAT" QUESTIONS

The "what" questions will be partially answered when you answer the "who" questions. You may want to consider whether these sessions would be valuable for a Sunday School class or adaptable to a couples' Bible study, in addition to the suggested women's study groups. Don't limit these studies to just one audience.

Also ask "What will be our format for each session?" These Bible study lessons offer a format that is workable for your study group; however, each group should adapt the lesson components to fit its needs.

"WHERE" QUESTIONS

Where to hold the Bible study meetings may be determined when you know who is coming. Many settings can be used for these studies, including a room at the church, a restaurant's private room, the lunchroom of an office, a community center, or someone's home. Once a location is determined, for maintaining the strength of the meetings do not change locations.

"WHEN" QUESTIONS

When will you meet for Bible study? What day will you meet? How long will the meeting last? How long will it take to complete this book?

These studies are planned so that each lesson can be taught in one session, for a total of eight sessions. However, if your group wants to meet for a shorter amount of time each week, the lessons could be taught in two parts, for a total of thirteen to sixteen sessions. **One and a half hours is a recommended time for each lesson** given in this series, assuming all lesson components are used in each session. Announce a planned start date and a final session date before beginning the unit of study.

The time of day for your meetings, of course, will be determined by the majority of the group attending and the availability of the space you have chosen. You may want to build in time for fellowship before or after the Bible study; however, remember that it is better to have the study members wanting the meetings to be longer, rather than wishing they were shorter!

"HOW" QUESTIONS

How will you promote your Bible study sessions?

You may want to develop a brochure, place posters in the church hallways, ask for bulletin and pulpit announcements, or use any number of creative methods for getting information to potential group members. Be sure potential members understand how and where they can become involved in this study.

Carefully consider these questions and any others you may have to establish the framework for your Bible study. Trust God to be there as you meet with other women to discover how to apply His Word to your life.

TIPS FOR BEING A BIBLE STUDY GROUP MEMBER

Each Bible study group member is important to the success of these Bible studies. Use these suggestions to help make your time together more meaningful.

- Agree to participate: The more fully each person participates, the more each group member benefits. Agree to study the lesson before the scheduled session, and agree to attend the sessions consistently to share the insight God gives you about each lesson. During discussions, contribute actively without straying from the discussion or dominating the group's time together.
- Respect each other: Through open and honest sharing we encourage one another. We can talk about who we are—our hurts, hopes, joys, and struggles—and what God is doing in us in this study. Each group member has valuable contributions to make to these sessions, and comments of each member should be honored.

- Keep a confidence: What is shared by other study group members during study sessions should stay as part of the group and should not be talked about outside study session time.
- Affirm each other: Affirmation strengthens the body of Christ. We can recognize what is best in other members of this study group and encourage them to develop these qualities as we grow spiritually together.
- Pray: Write down the prayer requests of other study members and pray for these requests during the week. Be aware that other study members will be praying for you.

Allow the Holy Spirit to work in your life through these Bible studies. God bless your time together with Him!

TIPS FOR BEING A BIBLE STUDY LEADER

As a leader, you have a determining role in the effectiveness of your Bible study group. Many resources are available to help you. Here are a few tips for some of your responsibilities as a group leader:

Demonstrate personal commitment to Jesus, the Word, and the people you lead.

As a leader, your personal commitment to God is of utmost importance. Leading a group of believers demands a strong personal commitment to God and His Word. Are you growing spiritually as an individual believer? Do you enjoy interacting with people? Do you want to see others grow spiritually? Then you will most likely be able to successfully lead a Bible study group.

Prepare thoroughly in prayer, study, and with a heart for the members of your group.

Use extra study helps if needed, such as Bible concordances, dictionaries, and study Bibles. Write notes in the margin of this study guide to help you facilitate discussion.

Decide before the first session if you will use every component offered in these lessons, or if you will choose only some of the components. See "Understanding and Using the Lesson Components" below for more information concerning each lesson segment.

The format for teaching these lessons will be interactive lecture, and group reflection and discussion. Be so familiar with the lesson content beforehand that you will be able to keep the group moving forward in the lesson. Ask each study member to read the lesson and write out answers before coming to the session so they will also be ready for discussion.

Facilitate discussion. Know your group and the lesson well enough to carefully select key questions that will generate interaction; resist the temptation to lecture.

Keep the conversations biblically grounded by sticking to the topic of each lesson. Move on to the next question rather than allowing silence, or "downtime," unless the silence is meaningful to the question being considered.

Guard a nurturing environment; encourage uplifting conversation, do not permit gossip, and insist on confidentiality. As much as possible, involve all study group members in the discussion at some time.

Always invite God's presence in your study sessions. Open and close each session with prayer, not as a formality but as a heartfelt necessity.

UNDERSTANDING AND USING THE LESSON COMPONENTS

You will find consistency in the components of each lesson of this book. An explanation of each component is given to clarify the purpose of each segment, enriching your total study experience.

CATCHING SIGHT
Introduction

The first component, "Catching Sight," directs the reader and study group to the topic of the lesson. Usually an anecdote or true-life story begins each lesson, followed by a brief explanation of the topic. Use these introductions to capture the attention of your group members as they are getting settled. If you are using this series for independent study, this introduction should help focus your mind as you begin.

GETTING FOCUSED
Begin your study by sharing thoughts on the following:

This component of the lesson initiates group discussion on the lesson topic. Break into groups of three to five to discuss the question or statement given in "Getting Focused." If you are studying independently, write down your thoughts on the question or statement. If you are leading a group, ask the group members to look at this question before the session and jot down some thoughts to facilitate discussion.

BIBLE READING

Bible passages selected to accompany each lesson are given in two versions: the New International Version and the *New Living Translation*. These two versions are side by side for easy reference during lesson study.

Shorter Bible readings may be read aloud by an individual or by the group. Longer readings should be read by group members before the session. Portions of the longer reading can be read during study time.

GAINING BIBLICAL INSIGHT

This component is the biblical exposition of the lesson. The pivotal truth of the lesson is given in italics beneath the component section heading. This is the "truth in a nutshell" concerning the topic of that lesson.

REFLECTING HIS IMAGE

This component gives an opportunity for creativity, as well as portraying the truth of the lesson. The Bible woman reflects the incarnation of the lesson's truths, and in most cases is given as an example of a life to emulate. This component can be used in several ways:

Individual devotional reading: Ask each group member to read this portion before coming to the study.

Small-group reading: Assign one person to read this component at the appropriate time in class or ask several women to read parts.

Drama: Assign women to portray each character in the Bible story and a narrator. Ask the women to give their practiced dramatic portrayal at an appropriate time in the study. Simple costumes will complete the effect.

Monologue: Request that one woman practice portraying the Bible woman in the lesson and present a dramatic monologue during the study.

EMBRACING THE PENTECOSTAL PERSPECTIVE
What is the Holy Spirit teaching me?

This perspective of a Pentecostal believer begins by asking, "What is the Holy Spirit teaching me?" We believe the Holy Spirit is a unique Person of the Trinity with a specific ministry in the life of a Christian. The questions raised in this component will help the Pentecostal believer apply the truths of the lesson in her own life.

INVITING GOD TO CHANGE MY VIEW
What change is God asking me to make?

After interacting with God's Word, seeing it in another woman's life, and discerning how it applies to one's own, there is one more essential step before we can live differently in light of the truth—prayer! This section provides questions that help each participant to go to the heart of the issue, asking God to bring change where it is most needed. Notice that there is usually a question provided to open the door for someone to receive Christ as Savior. A prayer is also included as a sample, a starting point, or simply as personal reflection.

JOURNALING
Take a few moments to record your personal insights from the lesson.

Space is given at the end of each lesson for writing down personal thoughts and reflections that transpire during the study of each lesson. The Bible study leader can take time for this in class or request that members complete this on their own time after the session.

AUTHORS

ARLENE ALLEN
—Catching Sight

The teacup collection that she keeps is a testament to the Southern hospitality one receives when meeting Arlene Allen. Born in the Appalachian mountains of Virginia, she never fails to delight and challenge her audiences with her quick wit and Southern-style wisdom.

An ordained minister with the Assemblies of God, Arlene is the director for the national Women's Ministries Department. She serves on the boards of the national Women in Ministry Task Force, Religious Alliance Against Pornography, and Global Pastors' Wives Network. She has an extensive speaking history that includes pulpit ministry, leadership training, and women's and ministers' wives retreats.

Arlene has been married for thirty-nine years to Gary R. Allen, who serves as the executive coordinator of the Ministerial Enrichment office of the Assemblies of God. The Allens are parents of two sons and the proud grandparents of two "incredible" grandsons, Grant and Jacob.

PEGGY MUSGROVE
—Gaining Biblical Insight

In her book *Musings of a Maraschino Cherry*, Peggy Musgrove talks about the role of a pastor's wife as sometimes like being the cherry on top of an ice cream sundae. But her life and ministry has been far more than just mere decoration.

Peggy is a speaker and freelance writer. Previously, she served as national director of Women's Ministries for the Assemblies of God and director of Women's Ministries for the Kansas District Assemblies of God. Peggy's written works include *Who's Who Among Bible Women, Pleasing God, Praying Always,* and articles for several publications. Peggy holds two bachelor of arts degrees, one from Wichita State University and one from Central Bible College.

Peggy and her husband, Derald, served local churches and in district ministry in Kansas before moving in 1993 to Springfield, Missouri, where they both served in national offices for the Assemblies of God. They have two daughters, two "utterly awesome grandsons," and one "fabulously wonderful granddaughter."

When she's not writing, Peggy enjoys many things—reading, playing games, family holidays and vacations, spending time with her grandkids and friends, traveling with her husband, and antique shopping.

LORI O'DEA
—Embracing the Pentecostal Perspective & Inviting God to Change My View

With discipleship being the passion of her ministry, Lori serves as the doctor of ministry coordinator and visiting professor of practical theology for the Assemblies of God Theological Seminary (AGTS). Previously, Lori served on pastoral staffs in churches in Decatur, Illinois, and Waterford, Michigan.

Lori was born and raised in Michigan and spent eight years in Illinois before relocating to her current home in Springfield, Missouri.

She shares her home with her awesome cat, named Zipper, who, she claims, can sail through the air like Michael Jordan. Aviation is one of her many interests and someday she would like to get her pilot's license. She's a firm believer that Mountain Dew, Doritos, and chocolate will be served in vast quantities at the Marriage Supper of the Lamb, though she has yet to find biblical support for her hopes.

Lori has spent a lot of time hitting the books and her educational credentials prove it. She earned a bachelor of science in missions and evangelism from Southwestern Assemblies of God University, and a master of divinity with a dual emphasis in biblical languages and pastoral ministry and a doctor of ministry in Pentecostal leadership from AGTS. In addition, Lori has served as a contributor to the *Complete Biblical Library* and *Enrichment Journal*.

CANDY TOLBERT
—Reflecting His Image

She may have been transplanted to Missouri, but Candy Tolbert is a California girl at heart. She is a woman who "thinks out loud" about her love of God, love of spouse, love of children, and her passion for seeing other women reach their full potential in Christ. A licensed minister with the Assemblies of God for twenty-five years, Candy is the national leadership development coordinator for Women's Ministries.

Her extensive background includes public speaking, Christian education, missions, university student ministry, children's ministry, and music ministry. She has written articles appearing in the *Sunday School Counselor, Spirit Led Woman*, and *Woman's Touch* magazines.

Candy has been married to the love of her life, Michael, for twenty-five years. Together they pastored several churches in the Southern California area. Candy is also the proud mom of two daughters, Rachel and Ashley. Candy's other passions in life include home decorating and good coffee.